T0305846

THE
ENTROPY VECTOR
Connecting Science and Business

THE
ENTROPY VECTOR
Connecting Science and Business

Robert D Handscombe
Eann A Patterson

University of Sheffield

World Scientific

NEW JERSEY • LONDON • SINGAPORE • SHANGHAI • HONG KONG • TAIPEI • CHENNAI

Published by

World Scientific Publishing Co. Pte. Ltd.

5 Toh Tuck Link, Singapore 596224

USA office: 27 Warren Street, Suite 401-402, Hackensack, NJ 07601

UK office: 57 Shelton Street, Covent Garden, London WC2H 9HE

British Library Cataloguing-in-Publication Data
A catalogue record for this book is available from the British Library.

THE ENTROPY VECTOR: CONNECTING SCIENCE AND BUSINESS

ISBN-13 978-981-238-571-0
ISBN-10 981-238-571-1

Typeset by Stallion Press
Email: enquiries@stallionpress.com

Printed in Singapore

Contents

Preface

For many years now, there has been an increasing emphasis in schools and universities to make the curriculum more relevant, to develop transferable skills and to increase the enterprise content of science and engineering courses.

This is to be applauded, but what about the science content of the courses? What we would like to suggest is that there is also real value in trying to connect science to business and that this should not be overlooked in the surge to connect business to science. Science, we suggest, is far too important just to be left to the scientists and our objective is to bring some of the fundamental rules of science to your fingertips so that you are more able to manage your business more successfully.

All of science is too large a prospect and we will be limiting ourselves to looking at disorder. We will be looking at how people in organisations attempt to manage, limit and avoid disorder. Most of our examples are from business, but our ideas are equally applicable in other organisations such as government departments or charities.

We use the word 'attempt' to raise the question in your minds that the task is not completely possible. You can try to manage disorder, but will you succeed? We raise the query with some certainty because there is a natural law at work that unremittingly changes useful energy into less useful forms and increases the state of disorder.

Scientists know about this natural law and some call it the second law of thermodynamics. They have also coined a word, 'entropy', as a measure of disorder, to help them define what is going on. We shall introduce entropy into our analysis and broaden its use well beyond thermodynamics.

We hope to show you that there is real science at the heart of management science. Managing disorder, ensuring creativity and innovation, taking risks, making trade-offs—all need to be done in the context of an underlying entropy vector.

What on earth, you might well ask, is the entropy vector? We can give our answer in two words. Read on. We hope that if you do, you will discover a way of making sense of seemingly unrelated business issues and be able to develop for yourself a framework within which to make future judgements and decisions.

Let us be clear: we are not saying that just one law of physics explains all management behaviour. Nor are we giving a set of rules that can be applied to all situations with the guarantee of success. The second law of thermodynamics on its own will not explain management behaviour and you would not be able to predict 'what happens next' by applying it. What we suggest is that by recognising the resonance between science and business, you will have a better grasp of management behaviour and a better chance to get the decisions right.

You may feel that 'entropy vector' is a curious and obscure phrase. But what did you originally understand by 'quality circles'? Was it something that could only be drawn with a good quality compass and a sharp pencil? And what about intellectual capital? A big city like Paris or Prague where philosophers gather?

Entropy is enshrined in the second law of thermodynamics and, as a natural law, ensures that life is varied, surprising and unpredictable. It forces us to expect the unexpected, and whilst the label that scientists have given it (the second law of thermodynamics) is a real yawn, entropy itself is anything but. In our experience, go-ahead managers say they find their jobs exciting. It is the excitement of entropy. Some managers, particularly in the sales department, see competition as the enemy. It is entropy, not the competition, that they actually need to worry about.

Entropy is the degree of disorder or chaos that exists or is created. There is a scientific basis to this and scientific links between effort, efficiency, risk and waste. Non-scientists may groan at the word 'entropy' but the other words—'effort', 'efficiency', 'risk' and 'waste'—are well known to all in business. We realise that for some, any science is too much science—but hang in there! There is no gain without some pain and we promise to keep it simple.

We have aimed to make the chapters stand alone so that you can dip into the book, although of course, you stand a better chance of following our discussion if you read Chapter 1, the signposting chapter, first.

We must all learn to manage and control change and there is plenty of social, technical and business change going on. In this book, we will be suggesting that a clearer understanding of entropy and the choices it presents will assist in that management of change—or, as we put it, in order to manage disorder you need to control the entropy vector.

The theme of controlling the entropy vector pervades the whole book. Go ahead! Find out what we are talking about. Take a trip along the entropy vector. Life will never be the same again.

Acknowledgements

A large number of people have helped us with this book and we acknowledge them publicly and gratefully.

We owe a big debt of gratitude to our daughters: to Emma for reading the first draft, giving us feedback, and for her continuous encouragement; to Isobel for her idiosyncratic typing; to Rachel and Ruth for their huge contribution to the cartoons; and to Sarah for her insistence on keeping the science simple and accessible. We also thank the rest of our families for their forbearance and for their general willingness to let us get on with our writing.

Thanks too to Robin Saunders, a thermodynamicist in the Department of Mechanical Engineering at the University of Sheffield, who patiently and constructively told us when there was too much daylight between our text and real science, and to Anthony Fretwell-Downing, our local business guru, who reminded us at regular intervals that business is more complicated than some of our two-dimensional sketches indicate, yet encouraged us to keep on with our simple pictures and hard questions.

We have drawn heavily on the ideas and words of others. We have referenced them in the text and in our 'Notes and quotes' sections but wish to acknowledge formally here their contributions. Isaac Newton recommended standing on the shoulders of giants and we have taken his advice.

We are most grateful for the support, guidance and encouragement of our publisher, World Scientific, particularly Anthony Doyle and our editor, Hee Tak Leong. We should also like to thank Nicki Dennis and John Navas at the Institute of Physics for their encouragement and advice and for the introduction they made to World Scientific.

The phrase 'the entropy vector' is ours. It was first scribbled on the back of one of our business cards as we discussed ideas and shared a bottle of St Emilion in the village of St Emilion. No idea could have a better start and we hope we have done justice to it.

All errors are, of course, ours and we ask forgiveness. All we can say in our defence is that in a book about disorder we suspect you would be disappointed if we got everything right.

Robert D. Handscombe   *Eann A. Patterson*
White Rose Centre for Enterprise   *University of Sheffield*
June 2003   *June 2003*

1

Disorderly Signposts

business success • socially responsible capitalism • leadership and change • excitement of entropy • signposts to chapters

Entropy is the degree of disorder or chaos that exists or is created. We might take a more detailed look at degrees of disorder later but for the moment this should suffice. So, in a book about disorder you might have hoped that we would have got on top of the job and have presented a signposting chapter clearly and logically. But entropy is powerful stuff and will not have 'neatly' and 'orderly' as bedfellows. So we compromise. The signposting chapter is in one place but the reference to chapters is not sequential.

Let us be clear from the start. This is not a rigorous scientific book. It is not intended to be and some readers will have spotted that from the first sentence because the definition of entropy is not rigorous. We are not trying to write a textbook. Rather, we are trying to explain some scientific rules in a simple and clear way and then make connections. We have found that these connections have made us more able to manage our relationships, our business, and our life more successfully. We hope you have the same experience.

Science, as we have mentioned already, is too important just to be left to the scientists.

We have also mentioned that the ideas that we relate to business are equally applicable in other situations and in other organisations such as government departments or charities. Whilst the aims of these other organisations may not be as focused on profit, money management, which at the simplest level is a matter of matching activity to cost, is often a common prime driver.

And they call this useful signposting?

So, this is Chapter 1, the signposting chapter. It is followed by Chapter 2 (surprisingly, you may think, in a book about disorder), which is entitled 'Planck's Inspiration' and which touches on the broad areas of nature, science, philosophy and business. Our guiding principle in this context has been to 'keep it simple' and we have tried to summarise where we have got to and remind our readers of what has been said on a fairly regular basis.

We keep talking about managing businesses more successfully, so perhaps we should explain at the outset what we feel to be relevant. We suggest three themes, the first being 'socially responsible capitalism', which provides long-term stability for employment and profit. However, entropy (disorder) exists and, as we shall find out later, it increases in all real processes and works against stability.

So, we must learn to manage and control change, which is the essence of this book in layman's terms. Since entropy militates against stability and since socially responsible capitalism is a blend of sometimes competing objectives, it is easy to see why success can be elusive. In this book, we will be suggesting that vector analysis is useful in looking at competing objectives—in the same way that it is useful in determining how to sail across a river to a point on the opposite bank when the current flows in one direction and the wind blows in another.

Secondly, we argue for a collective determination to embrace change. We say 'collective' in the sense that all the people in the organisation must be involved. This means that change should be 'bottom-up', or at least 'bottom on board'. This is not a cynical view but the realpolitik of bringing about effective change in an organisation.

Finally, we explore the courage to ask the hard questions. It takes courage from top management to ask fundamental questions about the business in an open way. There is a risk that it might look indecisive but, for a successful business, you need both leadership and the involvement of the rest—or, better, the fuller-blooded version of empowerment. The trick of course is to ask the right questions and to make sure that they are not too hard! Maybe universities should consider teaching a course to students entitled 'The Setting of Examination Questions'; for the skills learned here would have broad applicability.

We suspect that readers of this book will be scanning the pages for answers and instead will find analysis. We will answer in our defence in two ways. First, we suggest that answers alone are often quite useless.

There are, for example, numerous 'answers' in your local garden centre. By this, we mean that if your lawn has lifeless and brown patches, then the answer is a dangerous-looking spiky tool that you can buy. However, even though you have 'the answer', the problem is not solved until you learn to use the tool and apply that learning to your lawn. Secondly, we will say that in a surprising number of cases, analysis is the answer—learning how to discover and formulate the question is the fast route to the answer and we hope that some of the ideas in this book assist your analysis.

Entropy is familiar to engineers and physicists and is used in thermodynamics and increasingly in other sectors of science such as statistics. Our objective in this book is to employ some of the rules describing the behaviour of natural phenomena, the laws of science, to produce successful business strategies. We focus the science on issues associated with energy and its conservation and consumption (for example, Chapter 5); whilst the business issues being addressed are those concerned with creativity, innovation and direction (see Chapter 8).

We shall also seek to ask: 'Is entropy a good thing?' If you are managing a company, a division, a factory, a department, or just a small team, do you want to create entropy or find ways of reducing it? And, having decided which, how do you go about it? Long-suffering NCOs in the armed forces have a favourite saying reserved for those unfortunate officer recruits who fail to perform adequately: 'I would only follow you out of curiosity to see where you are going.' In management and at all levels, we must do better than these unfortunate recruits and ensure our staff know the direction in which the business is going and how their efforts will contribute to corporate goals. Chapter 7, entitled 'Managing Disorder', is about managing change and about techniques for good management.

We mentioned at the beginning that entropy is the degree of disorder. We have already asked some questions. Perhaps by now some further questions have come to mind, probably in a disordered fashion. If we shuffle them in to a logical order, we will reduce their entropy and expend some energy or effort at the same time. If next week we ask you to list your questions, then you will probably have forgotten some of them, and almost certainly you will have forgotten the logical order. This is entropy at work. It is always increasing and continuous effort is needed to keep it in check. You could expend more energy and write your list down, which would arrest the decay into disorder, but eventually the piece of paper would be lost and entropy would have gained the upper hand. We discuss these ideas of mental entropy in Chapter 10.

Our central theme is one of managing disorder and we introduce the concept of the entropy vector. Entropy itself is an engineering concept that arose from the study and development of steam engines during the 19th century. These engines brought about an industrial revolution and with it a spiralling demand for more power at lower cost. A hundred and fifty years ago entropy helped engineers to explain why they could not produce engines that were a hundred per cent efficient.

Some might regard it as engineers giving themselves an excuse for failing to design better machines. But, it is such a good excuse that they are still using it today! Over the decades, physicists have jumped on the bandwagon and used it to explain the state of the universe. Even the information technologists have begun to use it and today it plays a prominent role in information theory. We will touch on all these topics but the application of the entropy vector in business management is our main concern and the ideas of an entropy vector are dealt with in more detail in Chapter 4, entitled 'The Entropy Vector'.

Because there is a scientific basis to this book, we will introduce, as appropriate, the links to the scientists and philosophers who have led the thinking. Change requires time to be effective and Zeno, with his paradox of an arrow, will begin a thought process that brings us right up to modern quantum dynamics. But more of this in Chapter 6 ('Time and Entropy') and again in Chapter 10.

In discussing the origins of entropy in the 19th century, the names of Carnot, Kelvin and Clausius will occur. If we stick with Clausius's attempts to look at fundamental laws of the universe using the concepts of energy and entropy, what questions arise and what answers can we give? Clausius tells us that the total energy in the universe is constant and the entropy in the universe tends to increase towards a maximum value. We give an outline of what the thermodynamicists tell us in Chapter 2 and develop it further in Chapter 5, 'Energy and Entropy'. The 'Notes and quotes' at the end of Chapter 2 refer the interested reader to a rigorous mathematical analysis of the subject; it is not the intention of this book to get into detailed maths. Incidentally, notes and quotes occur at the end of most chapters. We give explanations for some of our sources and point to some of the books that have excited us.

Looking at the general economic picture, whilst inflation rates rise and fall there seems to be an overall upward trend. Is inflation a manifestation of entropy? This bears closer examination. A theoretical economic argument reveals that both inflation and deflation are self-correcting, i.e. part of a reversible system. But, in the real world, people and politics interfere and we end up with a real rather than ideal process, and in real processes, entropy is generated and is an indication of disorder. What kind of disorder might we come across in business? Inefficient production, strikes, unemployment, bankruptcy, irrelevant R&D? This idea is discussed further, initially in Chapter 3 and later in Chapter 11, 'Entropy Trade-offs'.

So, looking at an individual industrial process or an individual company, is the objective to reduce entropy production to a minimum? Does low entropy creation imply efficiency? Clearly, this can only be part of the story. If we expend no energy at all, the entropy creation will be low, the efficiency may be theoretically high but the output will be nil. Similarly, we could conceive of a system where an enormous amount of energy was applied for the given work output to ensure that the entropy creation was minimised. The search is for low entropy creation, low energy input and high work output, and you can join that search in Chapter 4, 'The Entropy Vector'.

Even now, the analysis is incomplete. In some parts of a company there may be a need for high entropy activity—unconstrained creativity is an example. In the 1996 UK Innovation Lecture, William Coyne, Vice President of Research for 3M Corporation, said: 'We are managing in chaos ... our competition never knows what we are going to come up with next. The fact is neither do we.'

3M could argue cogently against reducing the entropy of their research labs. However, it seems clear that the chaos that 3M claim to enjoy is of no value without their well-established, well-organised, well-constrained (i.e. low entropy) review and development procedures. More of creativity and innovation in Chapter 8.

Business is not without risk and we are not suggesting that there is a way to avoid it. Rather, we are suggesting that there are some preferred modes to deal with it and some important choices to be made as to which risks are taken. For risk and entropy, see Chapter 9.

We are close to a working axiom: You get the most useful output for any given energy input if you can keep an eye on what is happening to the rate of entropy creation. In short, you need to try and harness and control the entropy vector. We have already referred you to the chapter so entitled (Chapter 4, if you have forgotten) but many of the other chapters develop the idea. After all, this is a book about connecting and we try to connect. Often.

And in a disorderly way. Go on, have a look at some of the other chapters. This one is finished.

2

Planck's Inspiration: Nature, Philosophy and Business

Ockham's razor • Mother Nature • an engineering excuse for inefficiency • free energy? • the way you like it and for nothing

Keep it simple! Entropy will ensure that things are always more complicated and disordered than you would hope them to be, so the least you can do is to aim for simplicity at the outset. Actually, aiming for simplicity is also the most you can do as well. In this chapter, we will do our best to keep it simple as we seek to understand why and how entropy affects our lives. And if we want to keep it simple it seems appropriate to begin this chapter by paying our respects to William of Ockham (or Occam or Occum; there are various spellings of his name), who, back in the fourteenth century, set out some clear thinking on this subject.

Ockham, Planck and Mother Nature

William of Ockham was of the Franciscan order and taught at the University of Oxford. He applied his skills in logic to theological issues and was denounced by the Pope for dangerous teachings. He criticised traditional scholastic beliefs in intangible, invisible things such as forms, essences and universals and maintained that such abstract entities are merely references of words to other words rather than to actual things. So, keep it simple.

His name is applied to the principle of economy in formal logic, known as Ockham's (or Occam's) razor, which states that entities are not to be multiplied without necessity. Put another way, his famous rule is that you should not assume the existence of more things than are logically necessary, and it has become a fundamental principle of modern science and philosophy. It is called a 'razor' because the correct application of the principle enables you to cut out the irrelevant and unnecessary bits.

The difficulty in real life, of course, is that there are so many overlapping and interacting factors that keeping it simple and focusing on the priorities is never easy. However, beneath the tangled mess of real life situations, there are some fundamental principles that hold true. Max Planck, German physicist, Nobel Prize winner and originator of the quantum theory, was amazed and inspired by the way nature seemed to obey simple laws that were worked out by human reasoning.

Will we also be amazed and inspired? Let's find out. Let's look at two simple laws:

- In an isolated system, the only processes that can occur are those giving an increase in entropy.
- Achieving higher efficiency means reaching the given objective with less increase in entropy.

OK, so you are not amazed and inspired! Bewildered, maybe. Uninformed—well, just a bit, but fret not. On first reading, these statements may convey little, but we will keep coming back to them as we trace the course of the entropy vector. It will become clearer, as with early morning mist on a sunny day. We use the term 'system' loosely, and it could refer to a piece of engineering kit, a production line, a design team or an entire business; this allows us freedom to roam at will across a wide variety of activities.

So what about this idea of an entropy vector? The words 'entropy' and 'vector' are grounded in science and have specific and clear meanings. So, we had better start with some science ('Oh no sir, not science. Science makes me 'ed 'urt.') and with the natural laws ('Not law sir. Law is boring').

Most science students discover entropy when they begin to learn about thermodynamics and that is a good place to start. There are three laws of thermodynamics and they are usually expressed as negatives. It is as if Mother Nature were telling her wayward human offspring how the world works and perhaps the conversation would go something like this:

'Now look here, you lot, behave yourselves. There are no honest, short-cut, get-rich-quick methods available. You can't get something for nothing. There is no such thing as a free lunch or the perpetual motion machine. You can change energy from one form to another but the total remains constant and in everyday life there are always losses of useful energy.'

'And another thing—you can't get water to flow uphill by itself, or heat to go from a cold place to a hot place naturally, nor can you expect things to stay the same. They will naturally and spontaneously become more disordered.'

'Yes, and while we are at it, you will never hit perfection. You will never be able to get temperatures down to absolute zero in a finite number of steps and all other absolutes are equally unobtainable.'

'Right, there are your rules, now off you go and don't forget to tidy your bedrooms.'

Scientists of course clarify this and introduce Qs and Ws and Ss and differentiation. Then, by applying rigorous mathematics they derive expressions useful in increasing our understanding and harnessing the natural laws. ('Sir, maths makes me 'ed 'urt too.') Well, yes, we are all probably with our school class on this one and in this book we intend to keep the maths to a minimum, but you have to accept a trade-off. We can give you simplicity at a price. There is no point you saying 'Where did you get that expression from?' if you do not want us to develop the argument rigorously from something nice and simple, like:

$$E_a - E_b = Q + W. \tag{1}$$

And, if you do accept the trade-off, then you are halfway to accepting the entropy vector. By the way, the equation above expressed in words says that the difference in the energy of the system (E) between times a and b is equal to the heat transferred across its boundary (Q) plus the work done on it (W). This is one form of the first law of thermodynamics applied to a mechanical system; in essence, energy is conserved.

Entropy, engines and cycles

Entropy? We have imagined what Mother Nature has to say on the subject but we haven't introduced the term very carefully, so perhaps we should do that now. Clausius developed the concept back in 1854, though the actual name 'entropy' came later, again from Clausius, in a paper in 1865. Rudolf Julius Emanuel Clausius was a German mathematician, born 1822 in Köslin (now Koszalin in Poland), and was educated at the universities of Berlin and Halle. From 1855 to his death in 1888, he was successively a professor at the Polytechnic of Zurich and the Universities of Würtzburg and Bonn. Clausius was the first person to enunciate the so-called second law of thermodynamics—heat cannot of itself pass from a colder body to a hotter body. He was one of the first to apply the laws of thermodynamics to the steam engine.

However, to begin our story, we need to go back to 1824 and to a Frenchman called Nicolas Léonard Sadi Carnot. At around the time that George Stephenson was supervising the building of the Stockton–Darlington railway, Carnot was thinking about the design of engines. Following some elegant reflections on how to drive a piston using air as the working fluid and a heated block as an energy source, he described his conception of the perfect engine, the so-called Carnot engine, in which all available energy is utilised.

The air in the cylinder is heated by contact with the hot block and expands, driving a piston up the cylinder. As the piston is pushed up the cylinder, the block is removed and so the air begins to cool. On the down stroke, the piston recompresses the air, heating it, and if the block is put back in contact with the cylinder, the heat can be returned to the block. It became clear very quickly that no heat engine could be more efficient than the reversible engine Carnot had described. By 'reversible' he simply meant that there were no energy losses and that on the piston down stroke, the heat energy could be returned to the block as if nothing had ever happened.

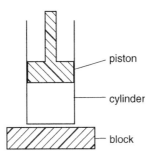

Put very simply, a block was used to heat air in a cylinder and then removed.

To continue our story of entropy, we need to make a slight detour. Carnot's ideas got people thinking and in 1854 William Thomson, who became Lord Kelvin, recognised that a consequence of Carnot's theorem could provide a basis for an absolute scale of temperature. Engineers and physicists still use the Kelvin scale today. At some suitable temperature, the block in Carnot's cycle will heat the gas, causing it to expand. At lower and lower temperatures, the expansion is less and less. This relationship between temperature and volume was already known from the work of Jacques Charles and Joseph Louis Gay-Lussac—as was the relationship between volume and pressure (from the work of Robert Boyle). Lord Kelvin brought these two relationships together with the realisation that, at absolute zero (0 K), pressure and volume must also be zero because the ratio of temperature to the product of pressure times volume must be a constant. A mathematician would write this as: p multiplied by v and divided by t is equal to a constant. When temperature is reduced to zero, the product of pressure and volume reduces to zero as well. One implication of this conclusion is that at absolute zero everything occupies no space. Absolute zero is, well, absolutely cold and, like all absolutes, not attainable in practice. The value of $-273.15°C$ was given to it at the International Weights and Measures Conference in 1956. Water freezes at 273 K and you are probably reading this at about 294 K or 21°C.

Now, with temperature clearly explained, it fell to Clausius to tell us something about entropy. He adopted Kelvin's ideas on temperature and developed the hypothesis that the heat absorbed by a body at a certain temperature divided by that temperature was the entropy change of the system. Now, for a closed reversible system, like Carnot's cycle, the entropy change is zero. Let's see if we can picture this. The heat passed by the block to the gas initially is exactly matched by the amount of heat returned to the block. So the net heat transfer or absorption is zero. Since entropy equals heat divided by the temperature, entropy must be zero because the net heat absorbed is zero and zero divided by anything is still zero. Carnot's cycle was conceived as the perfect engine and, like all absolutes, cannot exist. In real, irreversible systems, there are heat losses. Let us go back to Carnot's heat engine: it would become irreversible if we found that we could not return all the heat energy to the hot block. The amount of heat returned to the block would be less than the heat taken from it (a positive heat transfer) and, as a consequence, the entropy change would be positive. Real processes are associated with the generation of entropy. In other words, in real, irreversible situations energy is apparently 'lost' and this 'loss of energy' shows up in Clausius's hypothesis as an increase in entropy. Actually, the energy has been degraded, as we will discuss in the next section.

The degradation of energy

Lord Kelvin brought these ideas together in his principle of degradation of energy and we need to introduce one more technical term here, 'exergy'. Exergy is a modern term coined by a European, Raut, in 1956. Sometimes it is called 'availability', a term made popular by engineers at the Massachusetts Institute of Technology in the 1940s. Exergy requires no translation between languages and also has no meaning in other technical areas and so can be used without ambiguity. A much older term is 'free energy', used by early workers such as Hermann Ludwig Ferdinand von Helmholtz, a German scientist of extraordinary genius, and, more particularly, J. Willard Gibbs, an American mathematical physicist. The exergy of a system is the potential energy available to do useful work. Gibbs suggested that the useful work done by a system was always less than the exergy or free energy consumed and the difference was related to entropy. Gibbs' papers on thermodynamics were published in the *Transactions of the Connecticut Academy*, but because of their mathematical complexity and their appearance in an obscure journal, scientists in the United States did not recognise their value. However, in the last decade of the nineteenth century, translations were made first into German and then into French and his theorems became developed and used—though in Europe for some years before their importance was realised back in the United States.

What was Gibbs getting at when he talked of free energy? Energy certainly isn't free at the point of sale! He was meaning 'available to do work' and we might just take a final ride on Carnot's cycle.

When a process is reversible, all the energy that we supply (or exergy) is converted into useful work and no entropy is created, so when we reverse the system we can get all our energy (or exergy) back. But, when the cycle is irreversible the energy that we supply is converted into both entropy and useful work and, because entropy is associated with disorder, it cannot be converted back and some of our energy is 'lost' forever. It is no longer 'available', no longer 'free'. The more the entropy that is created, the less useful the work that is produced and the less efficient an engine becomes. Operating efficiency is the amount of useful work we get out of an engine compared with what would be possible if all the energy originally in the fuel was completely and usefully converted. The typical operating efficiency for a petrol engine is 20%; for a diesel engine or a gas turbine, maybe 30%; and for a steam power plant, about 40%. Not very impressive but it is the best that modern technology can produce. You are probably beginning to appreciate why we suggested in the introduction that entropy provides engineers with an excuse for designing inefficient machines.

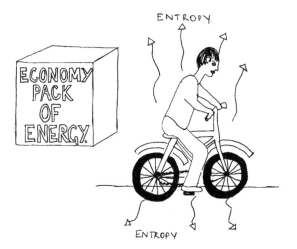

Exergy is converted to useful work and entropy.

By 1865, when David Livingstone set off to find the source of the Nile and the US was preoccupied with its civil war these ideas were becoming well established amongst thermodynamicists and Clausius deduced the two fundamental laws of the mechanical theory of heat. These are known as the first law of thermodynamics (the energy of the universe is constant) and the second law of thermodynamics (the entropy of the universe tends to a maximum). If the total energy is constant, and entropy tends to increase, then energy available to do useful work, i.e. exergy, must tend to decrease, perhaps to zero. This is bad news for us all. It suggests that there are finite resources in the universe and that they are not replenished as we use them.

There is more bad news. Entropic degradation goes on by itself regardless of whether the exergy is used productively. Systems and things tend to become disordered on their own without any help from us. We all know how the garden deteriorates into disorder when it is left alone, or how a kid's bedroom degenerates into a tip without any help. This is because every real process is irreversible. Steam rises from hot cups of coffee as they cool down, but they never heat up and retrieve the steam on their own. Papers can slip off your desk onto the floor but they never slip back onto your desk of their own accord.

Interim report

That's about twelve hundred words of engineering, so it's probably time to touch base on business issues, so let's summarise. We have talked about the first and second laws of thermodynamics and we can paraphrase them for use in a business context as (1) *you can't have something for nothing* and (2) *you can't have it just anyway you like.*

The second law of René Descartes? Literally, 'I create disorder, therefore I am'.

Of course, from the viewpoint of customers, they would both like something for nothing and to have it the way they want it. If a business delivered exactly what the customer wanted and for nothing, it would very quickly disappear, thereby satisfying the laws.

And what might the customer want? Free air fares? Even attempts to approach this are risky. Cheap airfares were pioneered by Southwest Airlines and are well established in the USA. In the 1990s, there were increasing attempts in the UK and Europe to provide cheaper air fares with companies such as Buzz, Go, easyJet and Ryanair, to name but a few. But life is not easy. BA announced in the second half of 2000 their intention to discontinue with Go (now part of easyJet), Buzz has been bought by Ryanair and companies such as Debonair flowered briefly and then died. The task is to deliver something closer to what the customer 'exactly' wants than the competition can do and at a price as close to 'for nothing' as is viable. The business moral must be: Don't start a price war unless you are sure you can be the lowest cost producer.

In the last few pages we have also introduced two new terms: 'entropy' and 'exergy'. 'Exergy' is the term given to well-ordered resources that are available to do useful or productive work. Engineers would assume exergy to be some form of energy but in a business environment it might be energy, capital assets, intellectual property or manpower. Entropy is generated by all real processes and is a measure of disorder. When one is thinking in terms of energy it can be useful to imagine entropy as a form of chaotic energy that, due to its disordered state, has a reduced capacity to be harnessed for anything useful. This idea can be readily extended to business resources. Take for example manpower, mentioned earlier. The available resource is the man-hours (at whatever skill level). In the process of running the business, if we neglect training or apply man-hours to non-productive ends, then there is waste. At its lowest level it is displayed as poor profit performance. More critically, it becomes uncompetitive performance and ultimately bankruptcy (possibly with strikes on the way).

Every real process uses up resources, converting them into waste and something useful. Some waste may be utilised in processes other than those generating it. There are countless chemical processes where uses have been found for products that initially seemed simply to be waste products of the main reaction. 'Recycling' has grown to be a major business in its own right. Indeed, who would call themselves scrap merchants when they could promote themselves as metal recycling engineers. Yet there is inevitably some waste—the ultimate waste, if you like—which can no longer support any processes and usually appears as energy in the form of dispersed heat or turbulence. All physical processes, despite any local and temporal concentration of resources or energy that they may achieve, contribute to the increased overall dispersion of turbulent or disordered energy. Entropy therefore irreversibly increases in the known universe.

Notes and quotes

- 'My original decision to devote myself to science was a direct result of the discovery which has never ceased to fill me with enthusiasm since my early youth—the comprehension of the far from obvious fact that the laws of human reasoning coincide with laws governing the sequences of the impressions we receive from the world around us.'—*Max Planck.*
- William of Ockham (or Occam) was excommunicated for his thinking, which contradicted teachings of the Catholic Church. His dictum, Occam's razor ('Plurality should not be assumed without necessity'), exhorts one to believe that simplicity is to be preferred to complexity,

that parsimony is more likely to reflect reality than its opposite. Ockham was an innovator and wrote at length. Those interested might wish to refer to André Goddu (*The Physics of William of Ockham*, Leiden-Köln, E.J. Brill, 1984), who traces the influence Ockham had in the development of natural philosophy and natural science.

- A helpful little book for defining terms and concepts thermo-dynamically is *A to Z of Thermodynamics*, by Pierre Perrot (Oxford University Press, 1998).

- There is no evidence to support the idea that René Descartes, French philosopher, scientist and mathematician, came up with the expression '*Coccitupo ergo sum*', though his proposal '*Cogito, ergo sum*' ('I think, therefore I am') did much to place him as the father of modern philosophy. For further reading, try Roger Scruton's *A Short History of Modern Philosophy: From Descartes to Wittgenstein*, second edition (Routledge, London and New York, 1995), which claims to 'present the history of modern western philosophy as briefly as the subject allows'.

- Those looking for a more rigorous and mathematical treatment might like to try: J.S. Dugdale, *Entropy and Its Physical Meaning* (Taylor and Francis, London, 1996).

- We refer readers interested in the area of entropy and economics to Nicholas Georgescu-Roegen, *The Entropy Law and The Economic Process* (Harvard University Press, Cambridge (Mass.), 1971).

- Cheap air fares? The story starts with Southwest Airlines, which began in 1971 with flights from Dallas and by 2000 was flying 57 million passengers to 57 cities all over the US. For a potted history, see http://www.flybudget.com/history.html

3

Life, the Universe and Entropy

vectors, pool tables and Isaac Newton • forces for change • inflation and pollution • physics and information • Isobel's message • Maxwell's demon

We have spent a little time in the last chapter introducing entropy and looking at its roots in thermodynamics. But before we move on too far, maybe some further thoughts on scientific laws will help and maybe we can introduce the concept of vectors in the process.

Isaac Newton studied at Trinity College, Cambridge, and when the University was closed by the plague in 1665 he spent his time at home developing calculus before returning to receive his Master of Arts degree in 1668. We need to begin by considering his first law of motion, which may be thought of for our purposes as a particular case of the first law of thermodynamics. The law states that 'A body will remain at rest or continue with uniform motion unless a net force acts upon it' and before anybody asks what the use of that is we should all reflect that there would be no snooker or pool without it.

Indeed, focusing on the pool table lets us see clearly what the law tells us. The cue ball is struck and off it goes down the table. Does it travel with uniform motion? No, it begins to slow down because of forces due to air resistance and the resistance of the table. Further, when it hits another ball or a cushion it is likely to change direction as well as slow down. All straightforward stuff, the energy the ball starts with ends up as a variety of other energies: sound energy if the ball collides with another, heat energy from the friction of passing over cloth and through air, strain energy at the cushions, and so on. Strain energy, by the way, is the energy stored in a solid due to its being deformed from its natural or equilibrium state and is released with the deformation.

During the whole event, energy is conserved, even if the useful energy (from the pool player's point of view, the kinetic energy of the ball) is all used up by degradation to less useful forms. Kinetic energy is the energy that an object possesses due to its motion and is equal to half its mass times the square of its velocity. In the process we have just described—the process of a ball rolling down a table—the entropy has increased because although energy is conserved, all the useful energy has been used up. The balls on the table will be more disordered than they were at the start of the game. Certainly the energy is more disordered, going from a condition where it was all in one place (the kinetic energy of the cue ball) to a variety of places (sound, heat, strain, and kinetics of other balls). The entropy increases as the free energy decreases, where 'free' means 'available to do something useful'.

We can also say something here about vectors. The speed with which the cue ball travels is important. Too fast and it goes on after hitting the target ball to collide with other balls, to the detriment of future play; too slow and it may fail to reach the target ball. The good pool player will tell you something else, namely that it is not just speed but direction too. Get that wrong and the cue ball mis-hits or even misses the target ball. This

combination of speed and direction (known to scientists as velocity) is
a vector. Any quantity that is defined in terms of both magnitude and
direction is a vector.

The interesting thing is to ask how this concept of a vector applies to
entropy. The basic laws of thermodynamics tell us that entropy is always
increasing. But in what direction? Some insight might be obtained from
another of the well-known laws of physics.

Newton's third law states that 'actions and reactions are equal and
opposite'. You jump on a bench and the bench exerts a force equal to
the one you are placing on it to ensure that you land on the bench rather
than jump right through it. Fire a cannon and the cannonball, weighing
a few pounds, travels several hundred yards whilst the cannon, weighing
considerably more, lurches back a few feet. So, how does 'vector' apply
to entropy? Perform an action to reduce disorder and what happens?
Disorder crops up elsewhere. Always expect a reaction in an unwanted
direction and, whilst you cannot do anything to prevent the reaction, sometimes, by taking care with the action, you can influence the direction of
the reaction.

Incidentally, Newton's second law of motion is about how quickly
something happens. If we asked a physicist to explain Newton 2 in simple
words, we might get something along the following lines: 'The accelera-
tion produced by a force is in the direction of the force, proportional to
that force and inversely proportional to the mass of the body being accelerated.' Our argument in this book is that the underlying laws of science
apply to business, so what about this one? Well, we all know how difficult
it is to introduce change into an organisation, so maybe we could paraphrase Newton's second law. We could begin by rephrasing the above
definition as 'the rate of change produced by a force is in the direction
of the force, proportional to the force and inversely proportional to the
inertia of the body'. If we now think of the 'body' as a business,
we have: the rate of change in a business is in the direction it is pushed,
proportional to how hard it is pushed and inversely proportional to the
inertia of the business.

Can we develop this further? The direction in which it is pushed is to
do with vision; the 'how hard' aspect is connected with leadership and
resources; the inertia to do with culture, attitude, procedures, practices
(collectively, let us say 'corporate age'). Thus:

A company's ability to change is determined by its vision multiplied by its
leadership and resources, all divided by the corporate age.

Change rate = Vision × (Leadership + Resources) / Corporate Age.

Write this up on the white board at the next strategy meeting. It has all the right management words in it and you have the confidence that this equation is grounded on a natural law.

Inflation, disorder and pollution

Well, we can see from the above that it is possible to make connections between Newton's laws and business. Newton's laws of motion are about forces, actions and consequences. They help to explain what happens when we do something. They are applicable in scientific, engineering, social and business settings. They tell the truth, but not the whole truth. For example, energy degrades into entropy without us doing a thing. We apply no force; we take no action; there is a consequence. There is continuous degradation and the degradation of resources is a theme familiar to us all.

> *Dad, can I have extra pocket money to allow for entropy?*

Money, for example, is a resource that has the potential to produce useful work and it is constantly degraded by inflation. So, we might ask, is inflation a manifestation of entropy? Simple economic arguments can be constructed that show inflation and deflation to be self-correcting, i.e. part of a reversible system. We have already learnt, in the previous chapter, about reversible systems. They are ideal and produce no net increase in entropy. In real life, the consequences of high inflation, such as recession, unemployment and social deprivation, are politically unpalatable and the system is not given the time to self-correct. Politicians need growth to raise their re-election prospects and so there is intervention in the economy. The full deflationary part of the cycle is cut out and a ratchet effect occurs. The politically desirable, irreversible system guarantees a net inflationary process. To paraphrase Gibbs: 'Entropy devalues free energy', which is exactly what inflation does to your money.

Continuous entropic degradation of resources implies that change is always occurring. In fact, the word 'entropy' derives from the Greek for 'changing direction'. Many business gurus have already espoused the concept that change is inevitable, and the behaviour of entropy guarantees that result. We can hardly blame them for backing a winner! The question is, how do managers in organisations most effectively go about controlling the rate of change and the effects of that change on the organisation?

The hard truths are clear. The behaviour of entropy ensures that the business environment is constantly subject to change so that businesses that do not respond will be overtaken and left behind. These businesses will become progressively less profitable and, ultimately, they will be out of business. The challenge is to avoid this outcome by harnessing change to your advantage, or, to put it another way, by controlling the entropy vector. The smart play is to use an understanding of the entropy vector to get ahead and keep ahead rather than argue that entropy is the reason that circumstances and the competition have overtaken your business.

The trick is to control the entropy vector and, as you might be beginning to suspect, this is not altogether straightforward. Entropy is the degree of disorder in a system, and a disordered system (a high entropy system) is unfettered and unconstrained. It becomes more ordered as the constraints on it increase. A well-ordered system, like a well-ordered office, has greater potential to do productive or useful work. So, we might think that all we need to do is to create well-ordered systems. Sadly, it is a little more complicated than that. When we create a well-ordered system, we increase its exergy and decrease its entropy and, at this prospect, alarm bells should ring in your head! How can this be possible, you ask? To decrease entropy appears to be in conflict with the fundamental laws proposed by Clausius. We said it was a little complicated. The answer is that whilst the entropy level in our system may decrease, the system cannot be entirely isolated from its surroundings, where entropy will be increasing. In other words, we may have created a localised pocket of high exergy and low entropy but globally we will have increased entropy. In simple terms, we have used up some energy to impose constraints that keep exergy in and entropy out of a local pocket. The constraints might take many forms; for example, the insulation on a thermos flask to keep the coffee hot, or the discipline in a platoon or team that enables it to survive in a chaotic or alien environment. The total entropy change is the sum of the change in our local system and the change in the surroundings or environment. This total will always be positive.

Thus, efforts to produce well-ordered systems have costs elsewhere and excessively 'well-ordered systems' have excessive costs elsewhere. When the 'elsewhere' is outside our immediate sphere of concern, the costs are frequently ignored, either deliberately or through ignorance. We will come back to the issue of trade-offs later, but a word in passing on pollution seems appropriate.

A common example of well-ordered systems and external costs is seen with companies attempting to make themselves appear environment-friendly, when all that is happening is that their pollution has been shifted elsewhere and out of sight. Electric cars generate less pollution in their local environment; instead, the pollution is created by the power station where the electricity is generated. So, using an electric car rather than a petrol one still increases global pollution. Pollution is a form of disorder because in general we cannot convert it into anything useful. It is not unreasonable to equate pollution with entropy.

Entropy and physics

Engineers began to develop the concept of entropy in their quest for more efficient engines. Later, physicists and the information theory community took it up. Physicists tend to be purists by nature and will be less happy than engineers about the laws of thermodynamics proposed by Clausius because in a strict sense they are descriptions of nature rather than explanations.

Physicists ask the hard questions. Clausius suggested that the entropy of the universe has a tendency to increase. So, asks the physicist, does entropy help explain the origins of the universe and predict its future behaviour? Is the universe an isolated system and does it have surroundings? Is there a continuous creation going on somewhere using up entropy? How did the universe get into a low entropy state in the first place? And now you mention it, was there ever a 'first place'? There are many unanswered questions and each advance in understanding tends to create more questions than it answers, which is perhaps another example of the tendency of disorder to increase, as described in the second law of thermodynamics.

Scientists such as Stephen Hawking have tried to provide some of the answers. Stephen Hawking is the current occupant of the Lucasian Chair of Mathematics at Cambridge, to which Isaac Newton was appointed in 1669. In his book *A Brief History of Time*, Hawking discusses the way in which entropy forms an arrow of time, because processes that involve an increase in total entropy are the only ones that can occur. So, if time was to run backwards your coffee would spontaneously heat up, which might be very useful. Sadly, physicists also suppose that the universe would start to shrink, which might not be so pleasant for those around at the time. Or, more flippantly, by the time your coffee had reheated sufficiently for you to drink it, the cup would have shrunk so that there was not enough coffee there to drink!

Brain hurting? Well, imagine yourself making a cup of tea, and whilst you are doing that, we will conduct a thought experiment to see if we can identify the reason for believing that an expanding universe is associated with increasing entropy. Imagine a kettle full of water, with its electrical heating element switched on. When the water is boiling, connect the spout to a small cylinder and piston.

The boiling kettle gives off steam,
The scientists here will stare and dream.
But those of us who know what's what
Will realise that the water's hot
And apply ourselves while the dreamer doodles,
To make some tea and boil some noodles.

The expanding steam possesses exergy and has the potential to do useful work. As the kettle boils, the steam will move the piston, which we can assume is doing useful work. Maybe it is driving a conveyor belt that is delivering sugar lumps to your teacup. However, if we disconnect the piston and cylinder from the spout, then the steam is free to escape. The potential to do useful work is lost because we cannot recapture the steam once it leaves the spout. The entropy of the steam increases as it expands, unfettered and unconstrained, out of the spout. This is somewhat akin to the expanding universe. The steam in the kettle and cylinder is constrained to occupy a smaller volume than the steam that freely expands out of the spout. The lack of constraints makes the entropy of the freely expanding steam higher than the steam trapped in the cylinder and kettle. The molecules of the freely expanding steam are able to take up their position with greater freedom than those in the trapped steam.

We can extend these concepts to solids, which have much lower entropies than gases. The molecules in solids are trapped in some sort of structure, making them highly constrained. Another thought experiment may help. Let us imagine balloons filled with helium at a garden fete. Each balloon represents a molecule. At the start of the fete, all of the balloons have been blown up but are trapped in a large net. In this state they will arrange themselves in some regular pattern and this is analogous to the state of molecules in a solid. At some time during the garden fete, the balloons are released and begin to float around the sky in an apparently random manner.

Netted balloons   Released balloons

This new state is analogous to the molecules in a gas. The exergy of a solid is thus much higher than for a gas; and the entropy for the gas is much higher than for the solid. But we must move on, for the study of entropy and energetics at a microscopic level is the domain of statistical thermodynamics, as opposed to the classical thermodynamics pursued by Carnot, Clausius and Kelvin.

Probability and information

James Clerk Maxwell was the first professor of experimental physics at Cambridge University. He was twenty years old at the time of the Great

Exhibition of 1851, which attempted to show the world the great technical achievements of the first half of the nineteenth century. Maxwell lived in Kensington, London, and supported some of his work with experiments performed in his attic. He was one of the first people to study statistical mechanics, which, in simple terms, looks at the probability of reactions and processes happening. If we go back to the garden fete and look up at the released balloons, it is much more likely that we will see them just floating about randomly rather than being collected in the sky in a regular pattern.

Statistical mechanics gives a mathematical basis for looking at processes where there is a move from a less probable to a more probable state. Thus, if entropy increases in an irreversible process, the probability of a high entropy state forming naturally or spontaneously is always greater than that for a low entropy state.

Look at the pool table we discussed earlier. If we begin by simply tipping the balls onto the table they will take up a random and, compared with the normal starting line-up, a disordered position.

There are many more random positions than there are ordered ones, so it is more probable that a random arrangement will occur. The natural drift from order to disorder is a move from the less probable to the more probable as well as a transition from a lower to a higher entropy state. In a dynamic market, that drift can be fast. In 1980, IBM dominated the computer industry. It was the industry's largest and most profitable company. In 1992, it returned losses of $500m. What happened here?

After delaying entry into the personal computer market, IBM decided in 1982 to mount a one-year development. They came up with a winning product. Within months, demand exceeded supply by a factor of eight. The competition sniffed hungrily in a dynamic market and, indeed, IBM's development strategy had contributed to those dynamics. IBM had used an external microprocessor supplier (Intel) without imposing any conditions of exclusivity on the chip used. They went for an open architecture and the use of the MS-DOS operating system of Gates and Allen's software. Other manufacturers were free to produce computers which used the same chips and which were compatible with the same software. The computer end users had the chance to buy IBM compatibles—computers that offered the same processing power and same software, but available without delay and at prices well below IBM's. Effectively, IBM launched Microsoft and generously boosted Intel. From being a dominant player in a market which they felt they controlled, they found themselves in free-fall in a substantially more disordered market.

With hindsight we might suggest that IBM could have entered into some exclusive arrangements with key suppliers—we might suggest that IBM was big enough to have bought Microsoft. But this is simply saying that they should have applied some constraints. In the language of our balloon thought experiment, this is just another net to restrain the balloons in a relatively ordered state. Without constraint, it is more likely that the balloons will form an unordered pattern and, for IBM, more likely that their marketplace will become disordered.

IBM is a nice big example, but what about the day-to-day life of a manager? We can't make the decisions for him or her, we do not have the information or the skill, but we can suggest that over-constrained systems cost a lot of resources to put in place and maintain. They are improbable—like the balloons keeping the close-packing shape they had in the net once they are released into the air. Allow for waste; allow for drift; build in some slack; keep it simple.

The greater probability for the existence of the disordered state is one of the driving forces behind the second law and continuous entropic degradation.

We have mentioned James Clerk Maxwell, but the star performer in linking statistical mechanics with entropy was Ludwig Boltzmann, an Austrian physicist. He deduced that the entropy of a state of a system was proportional to the logarithm of the probability of the state. There remains some dispute as to whether the values of entropy calculated by the statistical mechanics method of Boltzmann are the same as those derived from the equations of Clausius. We do not intend to enter this dispute except to highlight that the third law of thermodynamics can be stated as 'at absolute zero the entropy is zero' or, put another way, 'at absolute zero the thermal motion of the molecules is so small that only one configuration is possible'. This implies that the formation of this configuration is certain and has a probability of 1. The logarithm of 1 is zero. So, at least, at absolute zero the Boltzmann and Clausius approaches coincide. However, in other circumstances, suffice it to say that in qualitative terms the Boltzmann approach allows us to extend our understanding of entropy to situations where a purely thermodynamic analysis is not possible.

Isobel's message

The relationship between probability and entropy is employed by information theorists to describe the information content of a message. The argument goes something like this. Take a problem (for example, how to get from Sheffield to Manchester within the next two hours). When we have some information (you'll not do it by aeroplane, because there are no direct flights), the number of possible answers is reduced. With complete information we may well find that there is only one possible answer.

The quantity of information is related to the ratio of the number of possible answers before and after receiving information. So, if we can think of seven answers to the above question, after receiving no information there are still seven possible answers; the ratio is 7/7 = 1. The logarithm of 1 is zero. No information. With just one piece of information (there are no direct flights), the ratio increases to 7/6. The logarithm of 7/6 is a small but positive number (0.15). With a lot of information (so much in fact that there is now a unique solution), the ratio becomes 7/1. The logarithm of 7/1 is larger again (=1.94). Information scientists use a logarithmic scale so that they have a way of adding the information contained in independent situations.

Physics enters the picture when we discover a remarkable likeness between information and entropy. The similarity was noticed long ago, in the mid- to late 1920s, by Leo Szilard, a Hungarian-born American nuclear physicist, better known for his work on the development of controlled nuclear fission. We will meet him again when we do battle with Maxwell's demon. Claude Shannon, an American electrical engineer, rediscovered the similarity in 1948: 'Information must be considered as a negative term in the entropy of a system; in short, information is negentropy.' Instead of negentropy we could say 'opposite of entropy' or, as Leon Brillouin puts it: 'Every physical state is incompletely defined. We have only partial information and entropy measures the lack of information.'

Clearly, the useful potential of a message is zero if it contains no meaningful information. In such a state, the message will have no exergy and high entropy. The message is like our helium balloons drifting randomly in the air. We cannot get any detailed information about the balloons or their position—indeed, they are continually moving to take up new and unpredictable positions. Conversely, a message that contains information is like the balloons in the net; we know exactly where the balloons are. The entropy and probability of the netted state are low and we can readily obtain detailed information about the balloons. Shannon's mathematics gets a little complicated but his ideas allow us to extend the concept of entropy into new areas.

For instance, one of us wrote this chapter on a laptop computer at home, where there were occasional interruptions from Isobel, his three-year-old daughter. Isobel has almost no knowledge of the rules governing written language, so that when she was asked to write a sentence on the computer using the letter buttons and space bar on the keyboard, she produced a random set, as shown below:

qldmwjsdmdwndojsydmlqjiugfytavzx   pskdsd   fipafafllapkoqlk ndalkchoasunc cwswalppppoxkm qopfpsldml wjcoualcmalkidfkdocof posklkokmlpdmx pifcmcoocmfijyvji

The information content of this message is zero and so the entropy is high. By chance, the sentence above which tells you that one of us has a three-year-old daughter, contains approximately the same number of characters selected from the same set of twenty-seven as Isobel's 'message'. However, the sentence contains a lot more information because the characters are constrained to follow the rules of the English language. The entropy of the sentence is low due to the constraints imposed and due to the high information content. There is a very small chance that Isobel could have ended up with the same arrangement of letters in her message as in the sentence above, or with some other meaningful sentence. So the sentence is an unlikely selection and arrangement of the letters, thus giving it a low probability of occurring and hence a low entropy.

Entropy is an indication of the lack of detailed information that we have about something, and Isobel's sentence has high entropy. We know from our earlier discussion of engineering that to reduce the entropy of a system, work must be done (exergy must be consumed). So, to gain information we must consume exergy. If you want to measure the stock levels in your factory, then you need to expend resources and the more disordered your stock (or the more detailed the information) the more resources you will consume to make the measurement. We also know that by reducing entropy in one system entropy will be created somewhere else. There is no escape from the second law. In the stock audit, the entropy creation might be in terms of disruption to the production line or additional stress levels in the workers.

Enjoyment of life increases as we go from low entropy (boring, predictable) to high energy (exciting, unpredictable). There is a recurring theme in modern life of favouring diversity—greater freedom, greater choice, greater opportunity, but you can have too much of a good thing and with increasing entropy comes increasing waste. So, control the vector so that you can cope and enjoy life to the full but do not expect to defeat the physical laws or prevent them from working. The law of gravity is at work whether or not there is an aeroplane in the sky. Why does the aeroplane not fall to the ground? Newton's first law gives the answer. There are other forces at work, notably lift from the wings, that result in a net force acting on the aeroplane that takes it forwards and not downwards. Similarly, the second law of thermodynamics is always at work. The refrigerated display cabinets in supermarkets are kept cool despite the surrounding higher temperature, not in violation of the second law but simply as a result of the work done in the compressors to keep the temperatures low. Take into account the energy consumption of the compressors and the degradation of heat exhausted to outside of the supermarket and the result is that free energy or exergy has been used up and turbulent heat energy or entropy has increased—just as the second law requires.

Maxwell's demon

We mentioned refrigerators in the above paragraph, an excellent example of an invention. Surely, if we humans are so resourceful and so inventive and with the odd genius amongst us, then there must be a way to beat the second law? Surely, if high entropy is connected with high probability, then there could be an improbable but possible way of winning? The question is not new and is nicely visualised in the antics of Maxwell's demon. J. Clerk Maxwell imagined a very small demon near a microscopic door in a wall that separated two volumes of a gas, both at the same temperature.

Now, as we know, equal temperature means equal average temperature and in any gas there will be some molecules that are moving faster than the average (i.e. at a higher temperature; let us call them A molecules) and some moving slower than this average (i.e. at a lower temperature, and we will call these B molecules). The demon is told to open and close the door to allow only the faster molecules, A, to pass from left to right and only the slower ones, the B molecules, from right to left.

In this way, the demon can make the left hand side cooler and the right hand side hotter. The states have become more ordered, the A molecules are on one side and the B molecules on the other. Hey presto! Entropy has decreased in an isolated process. Heat has moved from an area of lower to higher temperature. The second law has been disobeyed!

This is a nice riddle and various approaches have been made to explain it in a way that is consistent with the second law. Georgescu-Roegen summarised a number of them and we will touch on just two. Our first choice is a well-argued approach by Leo Szilard back in 1929, where he claimed to exorcise Maxwell's demon by showing that it needs information about the molecules to operate the door properly. This argument was developed later by Leon Brillouin and others to consider that, in a closed system with uniform temperature, the demon would only be able to see black body radiation, i.e. all the molecules would look the same. The provision of information (or a torch with which to see the molecules) introduces an energy consumption to satisfy the second law. Leo Szilard saw that information behaved like negative entropy and his ideas paved the way for equating entropy with deficiency of information and the development of the shorthand term 'negentropy'.

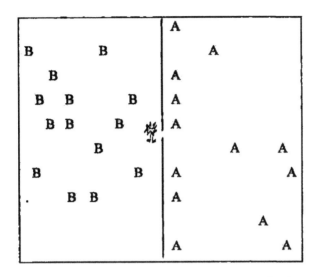

The demon allows the faster molecules (A) to move to one chamber and the slower molecules (B) to the other.

The simplest approach is to humanise the demon and consider that the energy it uses to stay alive and carry out its sorting satisfies the second law for us. The demon teases us, but he lives in an idealised world already known to be populated with weightless beams and frictionless balls. For the rest of us, the world is a place where the pool cues weigh something and the pool balls slow down as they pass over the baize. We will always find that when we consider the whole process we are faced with an increase in disorder and a decrease in useful energy. In short, the entropy of the system has increased.

And so to conclude . . .

This chapter has travelled at high speed through complex scientific terrain. Hopefully the journey has not raised your stress levels. Quite the reverse should have happened. We should have given you some detailed information about the remainder of this book and about the ideas that we wish to expound. This will have lowered your local entropy level by giving you detailed information, but at the cost of some consumption of exergy. Exergy, you will recall, is the useful work potential of a system. The consumption of exergy will have involved the creation of some entropy, or disorder, that will be greater than your local reduction of entropy.

The second law of thermodynamics demands that only processes with net increases in total entropy exist. Entropy is a measure of disorder. Fortunately, you consume very little useful energy and create very little entropy just sitting reading. But you need to eat from time to time and maybe the lights and heating are on. Work will have been done; energy will have been used to produce the food you eat and the electrical power to provide the heating and lighting, and in those production processes there will have been some loss of energy into forms that are not useful and some pollution. These are the manifestations of entropy. You are part of an entropy creation process no matter how quietly you sit.

The behaviour of entropy governs every process that we encounter, from the expansion of the universe to running a business or training a football team. The first and second laws of thermodynamics are about conservation of quantity and quality respectively and have applications in everything that we do. They can be paraphrased as '*you can't have some-thing for nothing*' and '*you can't have it just any way you like*'.

Notes and quotes

- Most people will have learnt Newton's laws at school during physics lessons. Some will also have encountered his mathematics. For those who missed out on this or who were bewildered, there are a number of good books for the layman. Isobel's older sister would recommend *Newton and Gravity*, by Paul Strathern, in the Big Idea Series published by Arrow Books, London, 1997.
- For more information on the arrow of time, see *A Brief History of Time—From the Big Bang to Black Holes*, by S.W. Hawking (Bantam Press, London, 1988).
- The concept presented in the section entitled 'Isobel's Message' is not original. Most ideas are recycled; only intellects on the scale of Newton's can achieve complete originality and even he suggested that if he could see further then it was only because he was standing on the shoulders of giants. Richard Dawkins, in his book *The Blind Watchmaker* (Penguin Books, London, 1986), expounds the idea in more detail but without the link to entropy.

- For a general background to the 'early days' of the development of information theory, try: Leon Brillouin, *Science and Information Theory*, 2nd edition (Academic Press, New York, 1960).

- Who knows the full story of IBM? It is considerably more complex than we describe here and we have simply used the IBM story to illustrate that disorder is a more probable outcome than order. Mills and Freisen give their own interesting perspective; see D. Quinn Mills and G. Bruce Friesen, *Broken Promises: An Unconventional View of What Went Wrong at IBM* (Harvard Business School Press, Boston, Mass., 1996). They suggest that 'IBM is making a comeback'. We wouldn't argue with them and maybe, by supporting Linux, IBM will enable itself to turn the tables on Microsoft and thereby give Microsoft the opportunity to enjoy the prospect of a dynamic and disordered marketplace.

- For a fuller treatment of Maxwell's demon, see: Nicholas Georgescu-Roegen, *The Entropy Law and the Economic Process* (Harvard University Press, Cambridge, Mass., 1971).

4

The Entropy Vector

uniting entropy and vector • sailing boats • Boltzmann index • lost in Bilbao and queuing in Detroit • taking control by letting go

In the last two chapters, we spent some time looking at the definition of entropy. We considered that in any real process, energy was used up and some waste occurred. In a thermodynamic process, waste occurs as heat and we generalised to consider other processes, including economic processes where waste took other forms. We also considered that the process was associated with an increase in disorder or, if this was not apparent locally, that even more energy was needed to keep the entropy out of the local pocket.

We also looked at the notion of a vector—in our simple example, it was a pool ball traversing the table, but equally it could be a boat navigating a river. One favourite type of school mathematics problem relates to determining the direction of ferries given the rowing speed of the ferryman, the direction and speed of the current and the assumption of a wind-free day.

The task in this chapter is to develop in clearer terms how the ideas of entropy and vector might come together in a way that will assist our approach to design and management problems.

Going against the flow?

We referred a moment ago to school problems connected with ferries and it is useful to extend the boating connection a little more. On a sailboat or yacht there is a little triangular pennant called a burgee at the top of the mast, which provides information to the crew rather than motive power to the boat. The tail of the burgee blows free in the wind and should point in the direction from which the boat has come, and if it starts pointing the wrong way—i.e. the direction in which you are sailing—it means that you are in trouble. In fact, so much trouble that if you do not take some pretty immediate action the yacht could well capsize. In simple terms, you can get the burgee pointing the wrong way by sailing too close to the wind and then sailing closer. The pennant points in a perfectly safe direction if you sail with the wind, except that the wind is not usually blowing in precisely the direction that you want to go.

Going with the wind (going with the flow) is the natural state but maybe undesirable from an economic viewpoint (you want to take the yacht somewhere in a specific time). Going straight into the wind is impossible unless you have the energy to do it. You might, for example, fit a motor to the yacht. Such 'lateral thinking' as this gets you out of the box, out of existing constraints, but such a step may not be possible. Clearly, it is not possible during the journey on the yacht and may not be possible before the journey. It requires time, resources, energy and of course a low entropy fuel input that gets converted into high entropy heat and waste.

In many situations, sailing close to the wind is the only practical course of action. It is the most efficient path given the energy and resources available. However, a good skipper will know that sailing too close to the wind—to get even greater speed or fewer course adjustments—brings with it the risk of capsizing, an extremely disordered, wasteful and high entropy outcome. The 'desirable entropy vector' is the one that concedes some speed and time in the interests of safety and minimum waste.

The above example indicates that there is no absolutely correct course of action. One skipper will set one course and another will choose something slightly different, based on his or her skill, the design of the boat, the assessment and acceptance of risk, and so on. Absolutes, like absolute zero, are valuable concepts and reference points, but the only thing you can say about absolutes is that they absolutely will not happen in normal circumstances. Absolutes like total quality management are exercises in absolute impossibility. But the concepts are seductive and valuable, so you (well, at least the TQM gurus) can get fat and rich from selling the hope. Charles Revlon, that well-known cosmetic manufacturer, once said: 'In the factory we make cosmetics—in the shops we sell hope.'

One of the good things about entropy is that it promises that you will not get absolutes. As the third law of thermodynamics points out, the temperature of absolute zero is unattainable in a finite number of steps. We can expand this to say that the 'third law of econo-dynamics' promises that you will not get to any absolute in a finite number of steps. We know something already about the law of diminishing returns and the difficulty and inefficiency of getting the last little bit out of a process. We must choose a course of action that steers between doing absolutely nothing and trying to achieve absolutely everything.

Careful choice of the entropy vector is the most effective way to get anywhere.

In nature, there is a constant tendency for order to turn to disorder. A hurricane can turn a neat plantation of trees into a tangled mess in a matter of minutes. Similarly, though over a longer period, a cultivated garden can turn into an unkempt, wild and disordered patch. Disorder, however, is a highly relative concept. Something is in disorder only with respect to some objective or purpose. For instance, aircraft from different carriers at a terminal may look disordered but, if arranged alphabetically by destination, may provide a more ordered way for passengers to make connections than separate carriers at separate terminals, which clearly suits the airlines.

We referred in the previous chapter to a statistical mechanics understanding of entropy, which depends on heat resulting from the irregular motion of particles and where thermodynamic equilibrium is the result of a shuffling process. Many parents of young children will appreciate the analogy of a gang of two-year-olds let loose in a toy shop. Once again, nothing will be destroyed but disorder will reign.

Boltzmann vs. Clausius

We have talked about entropy as a measure of disorder or uncertainty, and the branch of science/mathematics that goes some way to explaining this is called statistical mechanics. However, statistical entropy (i.e. entropy as explained by and calculated using statistical mechanics) has been the object of serious criticism since its conception and is not easily understood, even by physicists. This of course may say as much about physicists as it does about entropy, but the root of the difficulty lies in the step by which statistical entropy is used to mean something more than a disorder index (i.e. a measure of how likely or unlikely a particular state of disorder is to exist). Boltzmann came up with a famous expression:

$$S = k \ln W, \tag{2}$$

where S is entropy, W is the probability of a macro state (scientists and engineers use the shorthand 'macro state' to describe a specific combination of circumstances), $\ln W$ means the natural logarithm of probability W, and k is a constant of proportionality. This expression is carved on his gravestone!

We can also write down a mathematical statement of the second law of thermodynamics, based on the definition that Clausius provided back in 1865. This equation is

$$\Delta S \geq \frac{Q}{T}, \tag{3}$$

where Δ means change (so ΔS is change in entropy), $\geq$ means 'greater than or equal to', Q is the transfer of heat and T is temperature.

This equation was developed with steam engines in mind and so deals with heat transfers (Q) occurring at a particular temperature T and with a certain entropy change (ΔS). It tells us nothing about the absolute magnitude of entropy. On the other hand, Boltzmann's equation attempts to tell us something about the actual magnitude of entropy, but we do not know the value of k or the probability of many macro states except for a few special ones, like absolute zero.

Clearly, any acceptable definition of entropy based on order and disorder must lead to consistent values in both equation (2) and equation (3) in all cases. The question then is this: Does the Boltzmann equation (2) satisfy this particular condition? In the previous chapter, we demonstrated that they were equivalent at absolute zero, because applying both approaches results in a value of zero for entropy. But we have just established that absolutes cannot exist, so this does not help much.

However, let us return to our helium balloons at the garden fete. When you put them in the garden shed for safekeeping, there is only a little spare space. There are only a small number of patterns in which they can arrange themselves. Most of the patterns will look fairly orderly and regular because of the constraints of space imposed on the balloons. These patterns correspond to Boltzmann's macro states. Since one of them must happen, for the balloons have to be in some arrangement or other, then the probability of one pattern happening is quite high. For the sake of simplicity, if we assume five patterns are equally possible, then the probability of each occurring is one in five. The entropy according to equation (2) is $S = 1.609k_a$, where k_a is an unknown factor and 1.609 comes from the natural logarithm of 1/5. We have grossly simplified Boltzmann's expression in this example. Correct calculation of W would take us into complex statistics, a journey that is unnecessary for our purposes here.

Now, let us move the balloons out of the shed and put them into a garage that is much larger than the shed. In the garage there is a lot more free space around the balloons and so they can find many more patterns in which to arrange themselves. If there are a thousand equally possible patterns in the garage, then the probability of each one occurring is one in a thousand ($W = 1/1000$) and the entropy according to equation (2) is $S = 6.907k_a$.

The entropy has increased according to equation (2) when we moved the balloons and this is in line with our previous discussions because we have decreased the constraints on the balloons by putting them in a bigger container. The regular patterns that we had in the garden shed are still possible in the garage but they are only five out of a thousand, so the probability of one of them occurring is five in one thousand. These five patterns are rather special because they consist of gathering all the helium balloons together in a garden-shed-shaped area of the garage, leaving the rest of the garage empty. All the other nine hundred and ninety-five patterns involve the balloons floating around in the remainder of the garage, and most of these nine hundred and ninety-five will look very similar, i.e. disordered. The probability of the balloons taking up one of these disordered patterns is nine hundred and ninety-five in one thousand; or 199* times more likely than our five special ones.

Now, we chose a garage that allowed a thousand patterns compared with the five in the shed. If we had chosen a warehouse instead of a garage, the number of patterns would be greater, zillions maybe. With a warehouse, we are beginning to get closer to the discussion of physicists who would

---

* 199 is equal to 995 in 1000 divided by 5 in 1000, which are the probabilities of the two events.

talk, for example, of molecules of gas in a given space. Most of the balloon patterns in the warehouse will be disordered and the probability of one of our ordered 'shed' patterns is around one in a zillion. You have to wait a long time, effectively forever, for one of our special patterns to occur naturally. This idea is known as Poincaré's recurrence.

I said 'keep them safely in the shed', but no, he had to let go of them in a warehouse.

The question remains. Does this 'Boltzmann index' connect with the Clausius equation (3)? The thermodynamicist would ask the question very rigorously. It would go something like this. In addition to representing a probability of a certain state existing, does the Boltzmann index also give a measure of unavailable energy in a closed thermodynamic system? And not just any measure—is it so related to the state of the system that a change in the index varies with a change in the ratio of the increment of heat absorbed to the absolute temperature at which it is absorbed? Now, most of us might groan at this level of technical detail and even the most resolute believer in a unified theory of entropy must admit that it is not immediately obvious that the Boltzmann approach gives the same answers as Clausius's.

There is a further, philosophical difficulty. An index based on probability is, by definition, based on probability. It may be extremely more likely that one thing will happen rather than another but no course can be ruled out completely—there remains a finite if small chance that the unlikely event will occur. On the other hand, thermodynamic entropy concerns itself with irreversible processes. It is not more probable that A will go to B; the motion is irreversible. B simply does not go to A.

Yet, if we heat a gas it will expand (if the pressure is held constant), which is equivalent to moving our balloons from the garage to the warehouse. In our example of the balloons, we have already demonstrated that the Boltzmann index exhibits the right trends. The arguments are not completely rigorous—but our intention is to convey the significance of entropy and particularly its significance in management and business techniques, rather than produce another physics textbook.

We can infer from our arguments that if we deregulate a system and give it more freedom in which to operate, then we will see more disorder and it will probably never work as well as it did before deregulation. The 'big bang' in the London stock market is a good example and the crash of Barings Bank, one of the oldest in the City of London, demonstrated the consequences.

This inference is rather shaky! There are plenty of examples of companies that remove layers of middle management (and thus give themselves 'more freedom in which to operate') that actually then put in better, not worse, performances. We might also consider deregulation from excessive state control where the introduction of competition can provide both better and worse conditions, as can be seen from the developments in Eastern Europe over the last decade.

'Deregulation' results in more freedom, but greater freedom is not necessarily bad. The task is to move from too little or too much constraint to the optimum. The magnitude of the change is important but so is the direction and, as we have already noted, magnitude plus direction equals vector. The challenge is in setting the correct entropy vector.

To conclude our discussion on Boltzmann and Clausius, we should remind ourselves that the thermodynamic equation for entropy deals with differences in entropy levels rather than absolute values, and in certain circumstances, under certain conditions and within clear boundaries, the Boltzmann index is as good a measure of absolute entropy as can be obtained. Overall, however, there is a difficulty in measuring entropy and an uncertainty about the use of figures. Indeed, we would be disappointed with entropy if it did not introduce an uncertainty into its real value. The point is that there is a basic difficulty and therefore we should not get hung up on figures. The argument that we put forward is that there are preferred and non-preferred entropy vectors and we will develop this approach without being quantitative.

Lost in Bilbao, queuing in Detroit

After a business meeting, rushed for time, short of petrol, we were trying to make our way to Bilbao airport to return to the UK. In our haste, we took a wrong turn and ended up in the city centre. We wound down the window and asked a passer-by the directions to the airport. Neither of us speaks fluent Spanish but we got the distinct impression that he said that if he were going to Bilbao airport he would not start from here.

Exactly how difficult it is to reach a given destination depends on the starting point. We will go further. Where you actually get to depends on the initial course setting. A colleague, Peter, was recently organising an international conference and claimed that his guiding principle was anarchy. No rules, no organisation, no structure. Everyone should be free to express themselves without constraint. But people had to be invited, accommodation and seminar rooms had to be booked, money had to be collected and spent, political sensitivities had to be stroked. Peter was wise enough to know all this and an organising committee was formed and, from it, a very small working party of very committed members of staff. The committee met infrequently. It was used to stroke sensitivities and to keep its members informed. The working party met regularly and, outside the meetings, was allowed to decide the necessary details that enabled the broader objectives decreed by Peter to be implemented. The result was a very successful conference characterised by a feeling of freedom, informality and open debate. He had set the tone and the academic objectives and had fitted the organisational details as subordinate activities. It was a breath of fresh air compared with many of the over-packaged, over-constrained conferences on offer. In an 'anarchy conference' such as Peter's, where you get to depends on initial course setting. The 'practical current' of housekeeping (somewhere to sleep, somewhere to eat, bills to be paid) altered his course towards the fully constrained direction but his final entropy vector was a high entropy vector—consistent with the free thinking / creative environment he desired.

A course that sets out aiming at a controlled constrained event drifts even further in the constrained direction under the influence of the 'practical current'. The entropy vector will be low and creativity will be squeezed out. One final point: there will always be more disorder than you want in an anarchy conference. It is therefore advisable to have a decent contingency fund to cover the last minute realisation that you need an extra mini-bus or some temporary help at reception. And if you are running the programme for a day and expecting delegates or your committee to volunteer on the day to chair individual sessions, be prepared to chair them all yourself.

It is not just creativity that gets squeezed out in a low entropy system. There are other adverse effects too and a very clear example of this is available to anyone flying into Detroit airport. We chanced to fly into Detroit whilst writing this book. It is typical of a major, modern airport and our comments are generic. We compare the experience with flying off on holiday to one of the many sun-soaked islands in the Mediterranean or elsewhere. At such a destination, the plane taxies to a stop, steps appear and the holidaymakers bustle out of the plane, onto the tarmac, into the blazing heat of the sun and across to *arrivals*. It looks disorganised, there can be queues at baggage reclamation, it's hot, but it works.

Over at Detroit, the level of sophistication, planning and building is impressive. It is a big airport and one designed for customer comfort. The aeroplane lands, taxies over to a gate, the connecting tube is extended and the passengers walk off the plane into the airconditioned arrivals building without having to brave steps, weather or the fatigue of walking across the tarmac. Neat, or it would be if the number of gates did not match so precisely the number of flights. Potentially it runs like clockwork. In reality, with a few flights delayed, others re-routed, the occasional problem with plane maintenance or passengers at a gate, the airport can be a nightmare. You are booked on a connecting flight, you arrive at the hub airport on time and then, as the stress levels rise, you remain parked out near the runways and wait for a gate to become free. And as you gaze through the window it slowly becomes clear that those four planes out there are also waiting and are in front of you in the queue. This is a highly constrained, low entropy system but it doesn't work. Metaphorically, the airport manager is sailing too close to the wind and the vector is too close to zero entropy change.

'Welcome to Patterson Airport, where the local time is 23:33. We anticipate arriving at the gate sometime tomorrow.'

In theory, low entropy means high efficiency, but the design sought a level of efficiency that was not attainable in practice and the actual result was disorder, poor efficiency, bad publicity and doubtless high operating costs to sort out all the missed connections and consequent claims. Over-constrained systems do not work. The second law warns us that there will be disorder and we must plan for it and build in flexibility to deal with it. Think of the beautiful yacht beating close-hauled to the wind. It is a wonderful sight but if the skipper misjudges and moves too close to the wind or a squall blows in unexpectedly, then disaster ensues and she will be a wreck of broken spars and shredded sails.

If we return to the school-days definition of a vector, we will recall that speed plus direction gives a vector. In the two stories above we have focused on the question of direction. What is there to say about speed? The answer is not complicated, for we understand a great deal about speed from the everyday activities of walking, running and driving. First, different people choose different speeds to suit their own temperament, experience and physical limitations irrespective of any external objective of the motion. Secondly, appropriate speeds are relative. For example, 50 miles per hour feels slow on a clear four-lane highway, yet it feels dangerously fast on a narrow and winding side-road. And, finally, when you are not sure where you are or what turning to take, a careful, slow speed with regular reference to external signposts is to be recommended.

The final comment above links us back to direction and to our discussion of vectors. Whatever the speed we apply to a process—and it will vary with our ability and experience and with the nature of the process itself—we should also take care to apply an incremental approach. We should take time to check on position and direction at regular intervals (the frequency of which depends on the speed) in order to ensure that, if necessary, we make appropriate course settings.

Taking control by letting go

The incremental approach has an important role to play in that well-known practical application of management science—the approach called 'just do it'. In principle, it, is always worth identifying an objective and appraising the task of achieving it, but sometimes there are too many unknowns. How do you balance competing forces, how do you cater for the unknowns of new designs, what about the development of procedures for a new process and how will the people involved in this interrelate? In these situations, the choice is between analytical constipation (or, if you prefer, paralysis by analysis) and the approach of pure simplicity: just do it. There are risks involved in taking the simple approach and some initial analysis is essential for determining whether there are real health and safety issues. If there are, then 'just do it' is a very poor strategy. Otherwise, it may be the only way to make progress, but the technique that gives the best chance of success is a relatively low speed and an incremental approach, since this allows regular course setting to achieve the highest efficiency / lowest entropy vector available. On occasions, a big leap of faith—the opposite of the incremental approach—might just work, but it is a high-risk strategy and, in general terms, not recommended.

The direction component of the entropy vector is analogous to the aims and objectives of a project. The task is to decide priorities of wants and needs and to state the end point clearly, but with tolerances set as broad as possible. The entropy vector encourages us to realise that the task of setting broad tolerances is as important as setting the specific objectives. During his postgraduate research, Bob studied the slow combustion of hydrogen gases in a heated vertical tube reactor. The gases (fuel, oxygen and an inert gas) were supplied into the bottom of the reactor via an inlet manifold, which had to have an airtight secure connection with the reactor. Bob selected some flexible mastic, cheap and readily available in the laboratories, to do this. It worked satisfactorily. After Bob had finished his research, another student took over the reactor to carry out further research and decided very quickly that it needed to be assembled in a much more rigorous and 'professional' way. A new frame was constructed and the inlet manifold was attached to the reactor with a metal flange itself firmly secured to the new frame.

One of the difficulties in the research was to ensure that the conditions of temperature and gas flow rates provided for slow combustion. This was not always possible to achieve, particularly since a range of settings needed to be studied. On occasions, a full ignition would occur and the wave front would travel down the reactor tube with explosive violence. For

Bob, this meant a cup of coffee to repair his nerves and some replacement flexible mastic to repair the apparatus, since the force of the explosion separated the inlet manifold from the reactor. For his successor, it meant the complete re-assembly of the rig since the rigid structure contained the explosive force and the reactor itself broke. The new researcher had set unnecessarily tight tolerances on the design of the apparatus, with catastrophic results.

Bob looks for new ways to blow himself up.

If vectors are about speed and direction, is there a course where speed is maximised or at the very least optimised? The answer is yes, but it is difficult to predict what that course will be, largely because there are usually too many variables to allow an easy analysis. Take for example the task of sailing out of a bay when there is a wind blowing directly into the bay. Sailing straight out of the bay is clearly impossible (speed equals zero and direction/course setting is extremely dangerous) whilst to go parallel to the coast affords a speed that is high but orthogonal to the desired direction—in effect you get nowhere since the effective speed is zero, although the course setting is very safe (provided you stop or turn before hitting the headland that forms the boundary of the bay). The way out of the bay is to set a zigzag course and to tack out of the bay. The angle you chose for this tacking will determine the speed and direction (vector) and, for a given size of bay, strength and direction of wind, construction of boat, size of sail and skill of sailor, one particular course setting will be optimum. The sailor must balance the time he allows to get out of the bay with the risk he wishes to run in doing so.

Put this in a manufacturing setting and the choice becomes one of speed of production (productivity) versus risk of error (for example, quality of product). The actual course taken, for a given production facility, is skill- and expertise-dependent. With volume and time, a manufacturer becomes faster and as a consequence provides an opportunity to cut prices or increase margins. He is benefiting from what is commonly called the experience curve, which is simply the continuous resetting of the entropy vector. How is the entropy vector reset? Increasing experience enables tolerances to be tightened and the process to become more constrained and more ordered. This results in a decrease in entropy and a corresponding increase in efficiency.

We have spent some time talking about the entropy vector and using the velocity vector as a helpful analogy. We have also discussed the entropy vector in terms of steering a course between two competing directions, which for simplicity we can consider to be at right angles to each other. This creates a mathematical device, a graph if you like, that simply says that the two extreme directions are completely independent whereas any course taken between the two extremes has a component of both in it. Suppose we label the y-axis 'Theory' and the x-axis 'Practice'. Is there a particular course—and with it a particular entropy increase—that will give the greatest efficiency?

Indeed there is and the value of a good education is that it provides an understanding of the relevant theory and a training of the mind to be receptive to practicalities that need to be adopted. The theory is likely to offer an approach that is too constrained and which contains too many assumptions that do not hold true for all instances. On the other hand, a purely practical approach tends to give answers for specific situations and fails to provide a logical framework that permits extrapolation to new conditions or insights that permit process improvements.

Some organisational structures are much like theories. They are precise, logical, constrained and in practice far less efficient than they need to be. A colleague makes his money by assisting companies to export. In particular, he has developed contacts and an understanding of business practice for trading between east and west Europe. However, one of his favourite stories has much more to do with organisational entropy than east/west trading arrangements. His UK client was a medium-sized, traditional specialist steel producer and its specific difficulty in breaking into the growing new markets of Eastern Europe was the competition from other steel suppliers from Western Europe. Barry (our colleague) was convinced that his client made an excellent product but not sure that the potential

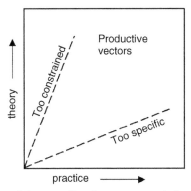

customer realised how good it was. So, he suggested the simple strategy that the company should not leave the selling to the sales representative but, rather, arrange for the top technical person in the company to travel with the sales representative so that the client could be convinced of the excellence of the product from someone who could discuss intricate technical details with their technical specialist. The strategy was almost still-born. The UK client had a very clear organisational structure and, with it, an equally clear operating procedure. Technical staff do technical work at the factory; sales staff travel to customers. The technical person had no experience of foreign travel. He did not even have a passport. The company had minimised costs and entropy but to the extreme of limiting its business opportunities. Barry's suggestion of a joint technical/sales visit involved him in obtaining passports and visas faster than the company thought possible and in accompanying the client team to the potential customer in order to support and assist the process. There is a happy ending. Not only did Barry make a good deal more money on this contract than he originally expected, the client convinced the customer of the quality of its product and won the order.

We have looked at the entropy vector in terms of mechanical processes and business activities. We should consider for a moment biological processes and note that the vector is important here too.

The sheer diversity of nature (a highly disordered, high entropy state compared with the simplicity of primitive organisms) indicates the ability of creatures to respond to new opportunities and conditions and travel a wide variety of entropy vectors.

Summary

Isaac Newton developed mathematical tools capable of describing motion and provided for those who could understand and use the tools, the opportunity to become masters of motion. Not surprisingly, this has led to a general faith in the arrival of a better world through the continuous and increasing application of knowledge and development of techniques. Technological progress has indeed given us a 'better world', or at least those of us with refrigerators, clean water and health care, but entropy destroys the idea that science and technology creates a better-ordered world. The second law postulates that matter and energy evolve in only one direction: from available to unavailable, from useful to useless, from ordered to disordered. We may duck and weave but we cannot escape the effects of the second law.

For any given system, entropy measures the degree of this evolution from order to disorder. Overall, the process is absolute, but, as we have seen in this chapter, there are options available to steer sub-processes and organisations. By using up energy we can provide a temporary, 'constant', low entropy system, which is highly constrained and may well be of value. For example, such an approach may well be justified and be very efficient for repetitive functions in a manufacturing plant. On the other hand, it is not appropriate or efficient for diverse activity and the need for creativity—for example, a design office. Neither is it appropriate if there are particularly adverse environmental consequences. Organisations and individuals have some choice over the particular entropy vector they choose and with it both the potential for efficiency and the responsibility for the effects outside their specific activities.

Notes and quotes

- 'Quality—the new religion—and its most notable guru, Dr W Edwards Deming'—so says Frank Price in *Right Every Time—Using the Deming Approach* (Aldershot Gower, 1990). According to *Management News*, Frank Price brings 'humour and colour into management texts', and you can get more of him on quality from his earlier book, *Right First Time—Using Quality Control for Profit* (Aldershot, Wildwood House, 1986).
- The absolutes of quality management? Philip Crosbie, in McGraw-Hill, *Quality Without Tears: The Art of Hassle-Free Management* (New York, London, 1984), identifies the four basic concepts of the quality improvement process, starting with the first absolute: the definition of quality is conformance to requirement. (The others are: the system of quality is prevention; the performance standard is zero defect; the measurement of quality is the price of non-conformance.)

- Those wanting a more traditional text should try *Total Quality Control*, third edition, and revised, fortieth anniversary edition, by Armand V. Feigenbaum (McGraw-Hill International Editions, 1991).
- For good pictures of close-hauled sailing boats, see *The Great Yacht Races*, by Bob Fisher (Cynthia Parzych Publishing, New York, 1984).
- Poincaré's recurrence is an eloquent illustration of Boltzmann's approach to the second law of thermodynamics. It states that the probability of different gases in two compartments returning to this state after the separating wall is removed is such that you need to wait for the age of the universe before it will happen. In effect, it will never happen.

5

Energy and Entropy

scattering the seed • organic companies • exergy conservation • energy management

The principles of thermodynamics make rather grand and far-reaching claims. We are told that energy is constant; entropy is increasing. Yet, in making those claims they leave a large amount of freedom to the actual path and the time schedule of any process or activity or event.

We can try, as Nicholas Georgescu-Roegen suggested back in the early 1970s, to find exceptions. On the one hand, he suggested we look at some simple and primitive living creatures that appear now as they must have done many millions of years ago. Surely there is evidence here of keeping entropy constant? On the other hand, he invited us to look at our inventive genius and consider, for example, how we make steel from iron ore and coal. Or, we might add, clear transparent panes of glass from a mixture of sand and crushed mineral. Both processes seem to be ones where we have reversed entropy from high to low.

So, how does this work? How can simple organisms keep their entropy constant and how can clever ones like us actually invent processes that appear to reverse it? And how can energy remain constant when we plainly use it up each time we take a ride in our cars? We are moving too quickly! We need to look at what exactly we mean by energy and entropy. As ever, we must look carefully at our definitions.

Law and disorder

The first law of thermodynamics demands the conservation of energy. The corollary of the second law is that entropy cannot be destroyed. Entropy is about the quality of energy, or its ability to do useful work. The higher the entropy, the less the value. We could say that lightning is high entropy. Compared with the output from a power station it is not very useful energy except for burning down trees that are past their sell-by date. From nature's viewpoint this might be more useful than a power station, but not from society's. We could say that coal and oil are low entropy. Their use enables a considerable amount of useful work to be done—though from nature's point of view their use may have been the cause of the pollution that led to the tree being past its sell-by date. There are always trade-offs in terms of money and value.

The first law of thermodynamics tells us that the energy in the universe remains constant. At first sight, this is one of those scientific laws that may hold true in the textbook but don't really work in real life. After all, we know from everyday experience that the amount of useful energy gets less.

We can read the cereal box at breakfast and calculate the energy that we are consuming and come lunchtime (or sooner) we are tired and hungry.

Time to replenish our reserves so that we have the energy to do something else that is useful in the afternoon. Where has that energy gone? The simple answer is that it has gone to two places. We have done useful work and we have generated waste. So, precisely what does the 'energy remains constant' law mean?

The thermodynamicists will get round the problem by saying that some energy (what thermodynamicists might call free energy or unbounded energy) clearly does get less but that this is matched exactly by an increase in bound energy—energy no longer available for us to use but still energy.

Since the first law of thermodynamics tells us that the energy in the universe remains constant, it follows that the energy in the universe is always conserved. So, when we are urged to save energy, what is really meant is 'save free energy', because if it is destroyed it cannot be recovered. It is a precious and finite resource. It should not be wasted. Alternative terms for free energy are 'availability' and 'exergy'. We introduced these in Chapter 1. 'Availability' was favoured in the US in the 1940s and 'exergy' by Europeans in the 1950s. The energy of the universe might remain constant but the names we use to describe various forms of it change pretty frequently.

All losses of free energy are associated with an increase in entropy. The more thermodynamically efficient the process, the less entropy gain and the more work from the system.

Thermodynamicists talk of reversible processes where the entropy gain is zero. Reversible processes are one hundred per cent efficient. In the real world, we can safely ignore reversible processes. After all, physicists also talk of weightless beams and frictionless balls but you will not be able to buy either in your local hardware store. All of these concepts are useful in defining the simplest arrangements to consider phenomena but these are idealised and unrealistic conditions. Irreversibility can be viewed as a lost opportunity to do work and thus the second law tells us starkly that there will always be lost opportunities to do work in real life situations. The real skill of entrepreneurs is not the clichéd 'never miss an opportunity' but rather the skill of selecting which opportunity to take. Opportunities will always slip through your fingers, but you do have some say in which ones.

We can safely expect in business, commerce and industry to find an increase in entropy whenever free energy is expended. The question we might pose is: How much of a measure of real efficiency is entropy?

Scattering the seed

Let us look for an answer to that question in a well-known industry—agriculture. If a traditional farmer has spent the morning broadcasting a sack of wheat on his field, then has he created a great deal of disorder and been inefficient or has he done as much useful work as possible?

It is easy to say that with a drilling machine he could have planted the wheat in straight rows (less disorder and thus less entropy) and with a tractor he could have done three fields and not just the one. However, if we include drilling machines and tractors we must also include the energy cost of making those machines. If we do that we change the equation. The farmer would have done a lot of work with relatively little direct entropy creation, but together with all those involved in making his machines and equipment, he would have used a great deal of free energy and generated a great deal of entropy. How has he used a great deal of free energy? In simple terms, the food and the fuel used by the people and machinery in the production of the drilling machine or the tractor.

So, let us not change the equation. Could the traditional farmer do more work for the same amount of energy dissipation?

He could certainly do less work! He could take great care to set his wheat in neat rows, one grain at a time, by hand, carefully, determinedly. Lunchtime would see him just as hungry as before and with a small fraction of the nicely ordered field completed. A low entropy process is not necessarily an efficient one.

He could run up and down the field throwing the seed willy-nilly, on the good ground and into the hedges and ditches, missing some areas and double-sowing others. Here there is greater disorder and he will run out of energy (and seed) sooner. Arguably, he has done the same amount of work but in a shorter time and with greater waste. A high entropy process is not necessarily an efficient one because he has wasted some seed, but it has cost less of his time.

There is, of course, another dimension for the farmer. As he walks down the field broadcasting the seed he can think about what he is doing and can practise a greater co-ordination of movement, a smoother action, a more controlled release of the handfuls of grain. The farmer can travel along his own experience curve such that, by the afternoon, or the next day or the next season, he can set a larger field in a morning's work than can the novice across the valley. A moderate entropy process (no attempt at neat rows but minimum waste as well) and a maximum amount of work for the free energy used.

In what way can the farmer use his natural resources (his energy and the seed corn) most effectively? The answer seems to be that by trading off the time put in with the acceptable waste levels and by applying mental effort and training to arrive at the most efficient mode of work, we have an optimum system—not one that minimises entropy, but rather one that has discovered the appropriate entropy vector.

A matrix analysis

Can we make sense of this through that well-used management tool, the two-by-two matrix? 'Matrix' is perhaps rather too grand a word. Essentially, we have a square divided into four smaller squares. On the x-axis (horizontally) we can plot one variable, for example entropy, going from low to high as we move from left to right across the page. On the other axis, the y-axis, we can plot energy, going from low to high as we move up the page.

To be clear, the energy shown in this matrix is the energy of the process. We look in Chapter 7 at the efficiency of the high and low energy managers.

The question is: What tags can we ascribe to the four boxes and does this tell us anything? We can see immediately that a low energy process can be associated with both low and high entropy change.

Low energy, low entropy might be seen as a minimalist, hesitant, go-nowhere strategy and at the limits it clearly is. However, get a little more into the box and it becomes a stepwise approach. One of making small changes (small energy consumption) and creating minimum disorder

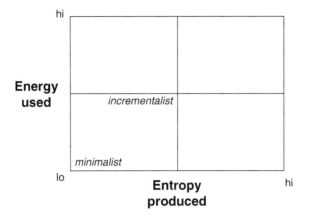

(small entropy change). Analyse the result, adjust and continue. This box is called 'step-*wise*' for a good reason. There is sound wisdom in small steps. We can consider logical incrementalism and incremental innovation to be features of this box and the incrementalist approach clearly belongs here. Mintzberg and Quinn have written much about this approach and many recommend it. This box encompasses strategies of continuous improvement and of high certainty development since small changes can usually be made at a considerably lower risk than large changes. This strategy works given careful and continuous management, although a company may need to have taken a rather more adventurous step initially in order to get a decent foothold in the market. Incremental change based on very low market share will at best give continuing low market share.

So a bigger step means more energy usage, more risk and in many cases the generation of a relatively high amount of entropy. We can call the high energy, high entropy box 'bite-size' and if all goes well the strategy will provide a viable opportunity. Richard Branson made a bite-size move when he acquired his first jumbo jet and began offering a new approach to the long haul flights across the Atlantic.

So, what about low energy, high entropy—clearly the terms are relative since the size of the energy change will govern the amount of entropy that can be created. In the limit, we get the highest possible entropy change if no useful work is done for the energy used. And an absence of useful work seems to be exactly what happens in badly managed incremental change—change because 'we need to be seen to be doing something'. There is low (or zero) efficiency, but an appreciable level of activity often obscures this. A busy office or shop floor is not necessarily an efficient one—and energy efficiency can become a fetish. Whilst wasteful, these activities are essentially low energy processes and maybe the bigger gains are to be made in reducing entropy change in a higher energy process. This low energy, high entropy box may be tagged 'distractive', because by and large it distracts from the things that really need doing. Of course, as the old saying goes, 'it is difficult to concentrate on draining the swamp when the alligators are snapping at your feet', but if possible we should focus on the big issues. To continue the animal analogy, our attention should be on eleph*ants* and not on *ants*. We might also say, our attention should be on training the sheepdog, not the sheep.

So, finally, the high energy, low entropy process? You might get there initially by skill, insight, luck and/or serendipity. Or, starting from a high energy, high entropy position, you might do it by devoting research, development and engineering effort. Either way the result is worth the effort.

Arguably, Henry Ford made a move to a high energy, low entropy system when he transformed his company from a jobbing shop with a range of different motors into a factory set up to mass-produce a single line. His flow-line innovation revolutionised car manufacturing and indeed the manufacturing industry more generally, but it was continuing research, development and engineering that enabled him to move into the centre of the box.

Low entropy means low waste and also high efficiency, and both are good news. Who wouldn't want to appear to be a low-polluting, environmentally conscious company at the same time as being the lowest-cost producer? This box can be tagged 'distinctive' and companies in it certainly are.

So, a matrix seems to make sense and, to recap, looks like the following:

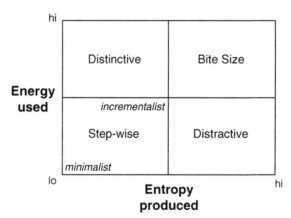

Organic companies

As we have already mentioned, two-by-two matrices tend to oversimplify things, and the above analysis ignores effects due to the size of a company.

It is easy both to think of small to medium-sized enterprises (SMEs) as a meaningful group and to assume that because they are not large, they automatically have informality, flexibility and organic structure—high entropy conditions that are said to assist in the successful development of a company. In practice, individual SMEs have individual characteristics that overshadow basic properties due to size and market presence, and medium-sized companies often show startling formality and inflexibility. Perhaps this latter is not unexpected.

Medium-sized companies (50 to 250 employees) will have arrived at their current size by a process of acquisition, growth or contraction. Given that acquisition will normally involve the incorporation of a company or part of a company that has grown from an earlier and smaller state, it can be expected that all medium-sized companies will have some track record in providing goods and/or services over a number of years. If conditions were stable over some of this period, then, according to Tom Burns and George Stalker, management practices might be characterised by specialisms; powerful functional roles; vertical management interactions; a command hierarchy and a complex organisational chart.

Burns and Stalker call such a system of management practices 'mechanistic' and contrast them with those required for conditions of change (dubbed 'organic'). Organic systems are characterised by a lack of formal job definition, lateral interactions and consultations and a greater responsibility for individuals to perform tasks in the light of their relevant knowledge.

A mechanistic system may serve a company well—and may be recommended for efficient running of a company in a stable environment—but what happens in the face of severe conditions of change? Why do firms not change systems in the face of new commercial and technical demands? Burns and Stalker concluded that the mechanistic system is not only a working organisation but also a political system and a status structure. As Machievelli pointed out long ago, there is nothing more perilous than to try to introduce innovation into a political system.

Companies that get stuck in a mechanistic system not only fail to innovate but also make themselves vulnerable to decline and takeover. Paradoxically, companies that have expanded by acquisition may well have taken on board management attitudes and structures which restrict further growth, since management systems in the acquired company that were inappropriate to continuing innovation and growth are likely to have contributed to the opportunity for the takeover.

We considered organic systems to be high entropy systems and they are certainly higher-entropy than strictly ordered mechanistic systems. But this conceals the key fact that organic systems are 'high energy' systems and it takes a strong leader to maintain an organic approach, particularly when some parts of the organisation appear to have stable conditions (where some mechanistic approach would appear to offer efficient management) and where newly acquired staff have a non-organic culture.

Indeterminateness and degradation

Let us look again at the first law of thermodynamics—or the law of conservation of energy, as it is sometimes called. The law tells us that the total energy remains constant, even if, during a process, it gets redistributed. We begin with a piece of coal. As it burns, it gives out heat energy—it might even boil water, raise steam and drive a turbine. At the end of the process there is a cold pile of ash where the coal was and the energy that has been released is spread through the system.

However, thermodynamic processes can occur at different rates and in different ways. The coal could, for example, be converted to coke rather than burned directly to ash. Nicholas Georgescu-Roegen calls this freedom and variability 'entropic indeterminateness'. This is a very important feature of real life and without this freedom it would not be possible for living creatures to appear to defy evolution. This freedom is also very important in business, for it gives an opportunity to do things differently from the competition and to create competitive advantage. Indeed, it also gives the possibility of reverse entropy processes, as in the production of the well-ordered product glass from the less well-ordered resources of sand and crushed minerals. Of course, the whole process is not one of net negative entropy if all factors are included, but there it no doubt that glass is more ordered than the mix of batch materials that went into the furnace.

In order to pull our thoughts together, let us take a ride home in our car. We arrive safely and note from the fuel gauge that we have used about a quarter of a tank of fuel. We also note if we touch the bonnet of the car it is hot. If we looked, we might find some carbon deposits on the plugs. Emission detectors on our route would indicate that we produced some gases.

What has happened here? Well, the thermodynamic process of combustion has produced some work (the car has taken us home), there is some waste heat (the engine is still hot) and there are waste products (emission gases and soot deposits). We know from the first law of thermodynamics that the total quantity of energy is unchanged, but there has been some kind of change. A quarter of the fuel is gone, for a start. The energy change is qualitative. Initially the chemical energy in our fuel is 'free' or 'available' and we can use it to produce useful work. In the process, the free energy is converted to bound energy—energy which can no longer be used for the same purpose and often has no further useful purpose.

Systems and structures where most of the energy is bound or unavailable have high entropy. Ones where the energy is free or available have low entropy (and high exergy).

The second law of thermodynamics tells us the entropy in the universe is increasing—and this is true also in any isolated system. The increase in entropy is met by a decline in exergy and the bulk of the increasing entropy comes from the release of energy from fossil (coal, gas, oil) and fissile fuels (nuclear). There is continuous, irreversible loss of exergy, a continuous and irreversible increase in entropy and, with it, an unstoppable transformation of order into disorder.

If we substitute our car for an old-fashioned railway train, we can easily appreciate that heat flows from a hotter to a colder body—from the red-hot coals in the hearth to the water in the boiler. This is part of the inevitable degradation of exergy and occurs naturally. We can picture a situation where heat flows from a colder to a hotter body; the domestic refrigerator, for example, but it only does this when external energy is applied. Switch off the electricity and the fridge stops working. Include the energy consumption required to provide the electricity and the overall process will have a net flow of heat from hot to cold, a degradation of free energy, a loss of exergy and an increase in entropy. This is all generalised by the entropy law, which is the second law of thermodynamics.

Rather disturbingly, the entropic degradation goes on regardless of whether or not the free energy is used productively. Buy a fresh set of batteries for your transistor radio, place them on a stone in the middle of the back garden and then, a full year later, fit them into the radio. You have had no useful work out of them but they are spent none the less. How do you get the most out of them? Well, for a start, do not store them outside in extremes of temperature and humidity. Other aspects of good practice may occur to you—in short, you are defining an entropy vector, a way of managing a process that gives the optimum efficiency and value.

In the previous chapter, we looked at reversible and irreversible processes and concluded that in real life only irreversibility occurred. Irreversibility is a general feature of all economic laws as well as thermodynamic ones. We are on the roller coaster, there is no going back, we must enjoy the ride (and, from a moral standpoint, attempt to leave it in a fit condition for others to use).

Consider for a moment the fantasy world of reversible processes. We would be able to get useable energy back into our car's fuel tank from the hot engine. At a stroke, we would need fewer supplies. There would be less demand. The balance between haves and have-nots would change in favour of the have-nots. We could feed more mouths by harvesting the entropy (the waste heat from our car, for example) and reuse it. This is the ultimate recycling. This is *the* sustainable environment.

Factories would be busy day and night producing weightless beams and frictionless balls. Everybody would be happy. The sun would always shine on holidays. Your favourite football team would always win. ...

The two products of the economic process

Engineers discuss the conversion of exergy to work and entropy. In an economic context, exergy might be factors of production such as physical assets, intellectual property or human capital. So, where an engineer might write:

$$\text{Exergy} = \text{Work} + \text{Entropy},$$

a social scientist would put:

$$\text{Useable Resource} = \text{Product} + \text{Waste}.$$

There is an underlying law. All natural processes are irreversible; all are associated with the consumption of exergy (resource) and the increase of entropy (waste).

Put another way, we can consider the economic process to be where low entropy ingredients are turned into high entropy outcomes. The economic process is one where there is a move from low entropy to high entropy (for example, the transformation in power generation of 'low entropy' coal, oil or gas into 'high entropy' electricity and waste products).

Natural resources are part of this equation but the economic process doesn't just happen; we humans apply skill, wit and cunning. Just how much cunning is for us to decide, since the economic process creates waste as well as a product.

Perhaps understandably, we all focus on the product we want and tend to ignore the fact that the other 'product' is waste. Waste is an inevitable result of the economic process and increases with economic activity. Companies strive to create products that are more cunningly designed than those of their competitors and the result is that we buy more of them. Look around your kitchen at all the gadgets and ask if you are cooking any better as a result. Only one thing is certain: all those gadgets use more exergy and result in more waste.

The crucial point is not whether we cook better but how we are using natural resources.

Green design

So, provided we do not have a major upset—like a global nuclear war or some unstoppable, deadly viral epidemic—it is reasonable to suggest that natural resources represent the limiting factor for the life on earth—certainly as we know it. Thus, the task is to deplete the natural resources as slowly as possible. The sun provides a daily supply of energy, but little of it can be classed as exergy, since we can convert only a small portion into useable energy. However, Mother Earth, or Gaia, has developed a number of effective ways to achieve this conversion, principally photosynthesis in plants, and plants, when they die, get converted by geological process into fossil fuels. These are nature's batteries, or stores of yesterday's sunlight.

Unless we learn to live within the daily supply, our society is not sustainable in the true sense of the word. We are depleting nature's batteries by using natural resources more quickly than they are being replenished. In terms of natural resources, we have been on a spending spree. It is an uncomfortable truth. Georgescu-Roegen puts it starkly: 'The best use of our iron resources is to produce ploughs or harrows as they are needed'. The iron is not available for us to make cars to get us to the fields (certainly not for smart cars to impress our friends).

Of course, going back to the myth of rural utopia is not an option and we would, of course, still want to use a good deal of iron to make the steelworks for our pharmaceutical companies, the equipment to ensure clean water supply … the list is endless. We would not trade our quality of life to enable some quantity of life sometime somewhere in the future for people we would never know.

But some of the thought processes are useful. Forty years ago, you could read popular science articles about the future opportunities to make protein from crude oil and thus solve the population problem. Nowadays those popular science articles discuss how to obtain gasoline from corn, oil from refuse, energy from biomass.

And pick up any rather more focused environmental news magazine and you will read that the demand for environmental solutions through the development of environmental technology will increase threefold in the next ten years. You can read forecasts that tell you that, by 2010, this market will be bigger than chemical and aerospace together.

Many years ago we were doing some consultancy work with a company that manufactured lead compounds for use in automobile fuel—petrol, gasoline, call it what you will. It was clear that there was environmental pressure against the use of lead substances and the threat that their market would disappear. In an effort to generate some creative thinking, we suggested that they consider catalytic converters as a potential diversification. It was a careless comment requiring too much imagination. Although motorists used their product, their customers were petrochemical companies. We were talking new products, new technology and new markets but instead of awakening them to the opportunity to think through what niches the environmental pressure might create for them, we invoked a defensive reply along the lines of 'we are basically a chemical company; we make lead additives'.

If our suggestion was a bridge too far, their reply was a bridge too short. They did not have the option of staying where they were because the environmental pressure was inducing change—they needed to face up to a steeper entropy vector than they had been used to. The situation called for an investment of exergy (resource) and acceptance of a higher level of entropy (waste). An ordered, efficient strategy was no longer safe. Setting a steeper entropy vector meant stepping outside the comfort zone. Life goes on; we now have lead free petrol but we no longer have a need for the products this company used to make.

In our search for 'green design' we have to recognise that the laws of entropy still apply—there will be trade-offs that must be accepted and unexpected disorder will sneak up on you.

A wonderful example came to our attention in the Sunday papers recently. A company—through either environmental or cost-saving pressures—developed a parking meter, powered by solar cells, for use in a sunny seaside town resort on the English south coast. A clever innovation, eh? Maybe each parking meter uses only a small amount of electricity but there is the energy and environmental cost of delivering the electricity supply to each meter. It appeared to be one of those developments that were good for the environment and good for profits too. Sadly, the design introduced a new constraint—it required no unnecessary interruption of sunlight to the solar cells and no one thought of telling the seagulls. They continued to perch on parking meters and relieve themselves on the face of the solar cells before flying off.

We began this chapter looking at energy and entropy and have ended it worrying about the environment. This should not surprise us, because there is a connection between them. Inefficient use of energy leads to high entropy production and the environment suffers as entropy increases. High entropy processes do the most damage to the environment. Fortunately they also do the most damage to a company's image, reputation and, because high entropy processes tend to be inefficient, they can also be costly and cause poor profit performance. In these circumstances, high entropy processes also do damage to a company's bottom line. So, there is sound commercial sense in being green. After all, green is the colour of the banknotes of the most affluent country in the world. This is not to say that the US has sorted all the problems but at least give it credit for colour-coding its currency to illuminate the way forwards.

Notes and quotes

- One text, more than any other, has stimulated our thinking in this chapter and is one that we have found useful elsewhere in this work. We refer readers interested in the area of entropy and economics to: Nicholas Georgescu-Roegen, *The Entropy Law and the Economic Process* (Harvard University Press, Cambridge, Mass., 1971).
- Henry Mintzberg and James Brian Quinn identify logical incrementalism as an important approach in business strategy, and we refer readers to pioneering work on this by Quinn back in the 1978 fall issue of *Sloan Management Review*.

- Niccolo Machiavelli, 'The World's Classics' edition of *The Prince*. Though he died in 1527 and wrote about the politics of his times (Renaissance statecraft and princely power), his message rings true today and in the business arena as well as elsewhere. Those of us charged with innovation and new product or process development should reflect upon his comments on page 21.
- Tom Burns and George M. Stalker, *The Management of Innovation* (Tavistock, London, 1961). The book combines three critical studies within the framework of an essay on organisational analysis. It describes and explains what happens when new and unfamiliar tasks are put upon industrial concerns organised for relatively stable conditions.
- P. Burall, *Green Design* (The Design Council, London, 1991). This book provides a useful set of guidelines for green design, including checklists for the designer.
- Bigger steps lead to greater entropy creation. Those interested in the science may find the following book helpful: J.S. Dugdale, *Entropy and Its Physical Meaning* (Taylor and Francis, London, 1996).

6

Time and Entropy

who created God? • entropy as the arrow of time • time management •
bored in transit • information flows • optimised production

One of the conundrums for religion is that if God is creator of the universe, then who created God? For some, their faith in God is sufficient; further questioning is meaningless. For others, there is an attempt to rationalise, and a certain amount of what might be called theological side-stepping takes place. In the Christian faith, for example, we might reasonably hear that God after all is eternal, without beginning and without end. But what if the universe itself is without beginning and without end as well? What if there is a never-ending sequence of big bangs and big crunches, to use the tabloid language of cosmology? Does a never-ending universe need a never-ending God to create it? Is the universe never-ending? Can that be possible?

We may know by faith but we cannot yet know by science, although quantum mechanics does start providing a scenario where such a continuum is possible. In the quantum theory of gravity, time becomes the fourth dimension to add to the three dimensions of space (x, y, z, or length, width and height), and Stephen Hawking has suggested that we consider it analogous to a sphere. Developing this analogy, we imagine time to be like a flea running around on the surface of a ping-pong ball. A continuous journey, without a beginning or an end. The 'big bang', frequently discussed as the beginning of everything, and the 'big crunch', proposed by physicists as how things will end, would be the north and south poles of the sphere.

The universe would simply exist. The radius of circles of constant distance from the poles (what we might call lines of latitude) would represent the size of the universe. Quantum theory also requires the existence of many possible time histories, of which we inhabit one. Different lines of longitude can represent these histories.

If you are not already lost (the analogy does not include a useful compass), then physicists would give you a final spin by dropping in the concept of imaginary time! Maybe it is time for the flea to jump off the ping-pong ball, but before it does, we can appreciate that it might move in one direction and then retrace its steps (or its hops, if you wish to be pedantic). The flea can travel backwards because in this concept of the universe, time has the same properties as the other dimensions of length, height and width and so it has backward as well as forward directions.

We promised at the start of the book to keep it simple and we have taken one or two liberties with the analogy. In particular, in describing the time sphere we have leaned rather heavily on Thomas Gold's time-symmetric universe, an idea that is decreasingly favoured by cosmologists, including Hawking.

Our simplified time sphere analogy has a certain appeal but it is not easy and if you have trouble with it, try thinking of a pendulum similar to the ones you find in grandfather clocks. Imagine such a pendulum swinging in a vacuum and with perfect bearings so that it never stops. At one extreme of its swing, let's say the left, is the big bang and at the other extreme is the big crunch. We are riding on this slowly swinging pendulum and time is measured as the angle of the swing from left to right. The maximum speed of the pendulum (which occurs at the bottom of its swing) may be considered to be the maximum expanded condition of the universe.

However, back in our real universe, if this quantum-mechanical description is true, how do we know which direction we are travelling in? Well, one answer is entropy.

Arrows of time

Stephen Hawking, in his book *A Brief History of Time*, proposed three arrows of time, which allow us to distinguish the past from the future:

(a) The thermodynamical arrow, indicated by disorder or entropy increasing with time.

(b) The psychological arrow, indicated by the chronological order of thoughts.
(c) The cosmological arrow, indicated by the expanding universe.

The thermodynamical arrow was discussed in earlier chapters. Clausius, who developed the concept of entropy in 1854, deduced that the entropy of the universe tends to a maximum. This is the second law of thermodynamics and governs all real processes, whether they are technical, natural or business events. If a process consumes energy, then some of that energy will be lost or wasted through its conversion into irrecoverable forms. 'Entropy' is the term used to describe the amount of irrecoverable energy generated in a process and is a measure of the disorder created by the process. Entropy is also an indicator of the degree of irreversibility. If a process is totally reversible, then you cannot tell whether it is going forwards or backwards, because the two directions appear the same.

The reversibility question was one that bothered Boltzmann (he is the one with the entropy formula on his gravestone) and he posed what is still considered to be a key question: not 'why is entropy increasing?' but 'why was it so low in the past?' The answer seems to be connected with the special conditions that created the universe and that, since then, the universe has been increasing.

If we return from cosmic considerations to the day-to-day world in which we live, we may note that no real processes are entirely reversible. There is always some entropy created, although sometimes it can be difficult to identify.

Let us digress for a moment and look at one such 'near-reversible' system, the hourglass. This was used by mankind for many centuries as a reliable timepiece and now occupies little more than a culinary niche for egg boiling.

The hourglass is a popular challenge and it might offer us a chance to check how our class is keeping up. So, how is it going, class?

It's all right, sir. Actually it is more interesting than we expected.

And the hourglass?

Dunno, sir. The sand seems to flow ever so nicely through the middle bit. Is there a loss of entropy, sir? Is it more neat and ordered in the bottom?

OK, class, listen up. The sand will run only in one direction in an hourglass: downwards. In the process a grain of sand loses the potential energy that it possessed in the upper glass by virtue of its height and mass. During its fall into the lower glass the grain gains kinetic energy by virtue of its speed and mass. However, some of the potential energy will be used to overcome air resistance and will be dissipated into turbulent energy in

How much entropy is there in an hourglass?

the air and become irrecoverable or lost. On impact with the bottom of the glass the kinetic energy is converted into heat and sound energies that are also 'lost' through dissipation into the atmosphere. In falling from the top glass to the bottom one the grain has moved to become in equilibrium with its surroundings, i.e. to have the gravitational force due to its mass counteracted by a reaction from the base of the bottom glass. It has moved from a less probable position, suspended over a hole, to a more probable position, sitting on the base. Transitions from less probable to more probable positions and towards equilibrium all increase entropy and consume exergy, the work potential of a system. In this case, the only productive work is to act as an indicator of time. The sand cannot run backwards and jump spontaneously back into the upper glass. However, we can supply more exergy by reversing the hourglass.

A clock or spring-driven watch works on the same principle. We wind it up and in the process supply exergy to the mechanism. This is stored in the spring by deflecting or straining it from its natural length. Engineers call this strain energy. The spring wants to return to its natural length and release the strain energy, so that it can be in equilibrium with its surroundings. The mechanism is designed to allow it to do this in a controlled way over a long period of time. The exergy is used to turn the hands on the watch face, and in the process some of it is dissipated into entropy mainly as heat through friction in the parts, but also as turbulence associated with air resistance when moving the hands through the atmosphere and as fracture energy through the generation of wear particles inside the mechanism of the watch. As with the hourglass, the useful work is in the form of indicating time, in this case by turning the hands. The mechanism of the watch will not run spontaneously backwards with the hands winding up the spring, because that would be movement away from equilibrium of the spring towards a less probable state and that requires the application of external energy, i.e. you winding it up.

We should now return to Hawking's second arrow, the psychological arrow of time, which indicates the direction of time by the chronological order of thoughts. Actually, this is simply a further restatement of the entropy arrow since our memory creates order from disorder as a mechanism for remembering. When your memory is in disarray you begin to forget the order in which events occurred, but more memorable events or recent events tend to be kept in order. So, for instance, you know that you got up this morning and then had breakfast—or, if you were lucky, it was the other way round! You might assume you had breakfast two years ago last Tuesday, but it is doubtful whether you actually remember it [unless of course that was the time you got it in bed]. The process of creating order in your mind uses exergy by burning carbohydrate eaten, for instance at breakfast, and generates waste products that contain less exergy than the food. Energy is dissipated somewhere along the line and entropy created. Of course, you can minimise energy usage. You could lie in bed all day, as many parents find their teenage offspring do, but energy continues to be used, by breathing and thinking, if nothing else. Not even the laziest of teenagers can recycle energy inside their body. So life itself needs a continual replenishment of exergy, some of which is used in the fight against entropy in your memory banks and hence provides an ever-present indicator of the direction of time.

'Time flies like an arrow; fruit flies like a banana.'—Groucho Marx

Finally, what about (c), the cosmological arrow of time? Most of us are unaware of this arrow of time, since we are not in a position to observe the expansion of the universe in any conscious way. However, astronomers and physicists can demonstrate quite simply some of the implications of an expanding universe. Take for example the movement of stars. An expanding universe would have us believe that the stars must be moving away from each other and, of course, that means moving away from us. From ordinary observations on earth, physicists will tell us that light that is moving away is subject to the Doppler effect. This makes the light appear red, because the movement produces an apparent lengthening of the wavelength of the light so that the long wavelengths dominate. Red is at the long wavelength end of the visible spectrum, blue at the short end. A similar effect causes the pitch of the whistle of a high-speed train to shift as it passes through a station. So, when we look at the stars, we should expect the Doppler effect to be there. We should observe far more red stars than blue ones and indeed this is the case. We can reasonably assume therefore that observations on a cosmic scale can help us to define the direction of time. If we started travelling backwards in time, we would expect to see the universe contracting and to observe more blue stars than red ones.

Time running backwards?

So time and entropy appear to be inextricably linked together. Returning to our analogy of a slow-swinging pendulum, it has constant energy, but the exergy is equivalent to the potential energy of the pendulum, which is a maximum at the extremes. Entropy is equivalent to the kinetic energy and is a maximum at the bottom of the swing. Of course, energy is conserved and, on the upswing to the extreme right position, the pendulum begins to slow down and kinetic energy is converted back to potential energy. In our analogy, time will appear to be running backwards because entropy will be decreasing. This is beyond our comprehension and the laws of physics as we know them would be distorted. Arguably we could not exist, as both physically and mentally we need entropic degradation to sustain life.

How is any of this useful in business management? Maybe we could make our deliveries of finished goods in a time machine to ensure that we always got them to the customer on time? The potential seems limited only by our imagination, but for the time being at least, such fundamental changes in the way things work will have to remain in the realms of science fiction. In the four-dimensional space hinted at above, physicists believe that everything is constrained to move in straight lines, which may appear as curves in three-dimensional space. This is rather like watching the shadow of a low-flying aircraft as it disturbs your walk in the hills on a sunny afternoon. The pilot is flying the aircraft in a straight line through the air (which, as we know, is three-dimensional space), yet its shadow on the hillside inhabits a two-dimensional world and appears to bounce around following the contours of the hills. The shadow not only fails to fly in a straight line but it also changes its speed.

We can extend this to time. In the example above, some people might be persuaded into believing that the aircraft was flying in a series of curves and rapid accelerations, because this appears to be the case when we view its projection onto the hillside, but we know that it is not so and

Look, Dad, the aeroplane's shadow is having a very bumpy ride

if we look up into the sky we can see the steady straight-line progress of the jet. In the same way, we know that time runs in a straight line at a constant speed. (Actually, we are required to accept from Einstein's laws of relativity that this is not the case if you are moving at close to the speed of light. Given that we are earthbound and such speeds are beyond us, we are stuck with time running in a straight line at a constant speed.) Yet there are occasions when we want to make it appear that time has slowed down in order to allow us to complete a task or to enjoy the moment, and/or to speed up so that we can go home! Traditionally, business gurus refer to time management. They invariably mean task management, but perhaps there is a time issue here. Perhaps it is our perception of time that needs to be managed!

Since entropy is the key indicator of the direction of time, we should work on the entropy of a task (or system) if we want to manage time. The

laws of thermodynamics tell us that entropy is always increasing and we
know from personal experience that time always runs forwards. If we want
time to appear to slow down or to stand still, then we must decrease the
entropy change in our project. Maybe if we can control the entropy of our
local situation so that its rate of increase is less than that of the surrounding world, we can have the effect of time passing slowly. Put another way,
we achieve in a short period of time what would have taken longer had we
not controlled the entropy. For example, take your paperwork into a quiet
room and spread it out neatly in front of you. No interruptions, no distractions, just you finishing off the work. It is a question of how we manage our own entropy vector.

Our definition of the entropy vector is based in the entropy–time
domain. A value of entropy at a specific time is a scalar quantity, i.e. it has
only magnitude; but the value and rate of change of entropy is a vector
quantity. A vector quantity has both direction and magnitude. So, for
instance, the speed of a ship in the Atlantic is a scalar quantity; we only
know that it is going at, say, 17 knots.

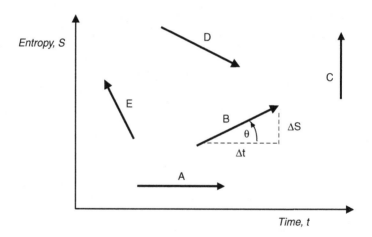

If we also know its direction, for instance westwards on a compass
bearing of 270°, then the course, given as 270°, 17 knots, is a vector quantity containing both direction and magnitude information. Forces are vectors because they act in a specified direction and with a particular value.
In the case of the entropy vector the direction in time is specified together
with the current value. Some examples are shown in the figure above.

Vector A indicates no change in entropy with time. This is a reversible
process in which no entropy is created, and all the exergy consumed to

generate useful work can be regenerated by reversing the process and applying the work. This is an idealised condition; let us move on. Vector B is the common state of affairs in which entropy is generated during a process. Natural entropic degradation has a vector such as B, but with a small angle, θ, to the horizontal axis. Vector C represents another ideal situation, for here an event is generating entropy but doing so instantaneously, since the vector is vertical and no time is elapsing. Vector D cannot occur on its own, because entropy is being destroyed which can only occur locally within a pocket. Vector D can only exist as a local effect and must be accompanied by a total entropy change (i.e. local plus surroundings) with a vector of the form of B. Finally, vector E involves time running backwards, which is not possible in the universe as we know it.

In the above diagram, the length of all the vectors is the same, but of course this need not be so. Not all ships travel across the Atlantic at 17 knots and if we were to plot a vector for a particular process then it would have starting and end points and hence a defined length on the plot. Our difficulty is that whilst we know how to measure time, we do not know how to measure disorder, or entropy. Thermodynamicists can calculate the entropy change in a mechanical event based on the temperature changes and heat transfers that occur during the event. ΔS equals ΔQ divided by T, they would say, and they could go on to show for example that cooling a slab of hot steel in a series of steps results in less entropy loss than doing the cooling all in one go. The thermodynamicists also have books of tables giving the entropy value for steam at various temperatures and pressures. These were constructed by hand calculations before the age of computers, simply because steam used to be the working fluid in most engines and is still the working fluid in most power stations.

All fine and dandy if you need to know about changes in processing conditions in a power station, but in business we are not so fortunate and we cannot define our precise position in the diagram, either before or after an event or process. The time axis is straightforward but the entropy axis is problematic. We do not know, in absolute terms, how much disorder exists at any instance. However, we are pretty good at estimating whether it has increased or decreased during an event and by how much compared with some other event. In fact this is close to the situation for engineers. An engineer would find it difficult to tell you the amount of entropy present in a pile of coal waiting to be burnt in a power station, but would be quite happy calculating the entropy changes occurring in the power station. It is easier to deal with changes in entropy than with absolute quantities.

Bored in transit

Before we recapped on the definition of the entropy vector, we suggested that there might be some value in managing our entropy vector in order to get more done in a given time. We need to work on the entropy of a task or situation if we want to manage time.

Let us begin by seeing what we can learn from our own perceptions of time. Time appears to pass relatively quickly when we are engaged in an activity that we enjoy or that totally engages us. Time passes very slowly when we are inactive and bored. When you have a five-hour delay on your flight in a small airport with one waiting area, your boredom level rises rapidly and with it your frustration with the airline and airport authorities. The frustration tends to lead to disordered thinking, which wastes exergy, and time seems to pass slowly. Entropy creation is high (large ΔS) and for any given time interval (Δt) the angle, θ, is relatively large, giving us a steep vector. Our perception is that time has passed slowly, because normally we would not have reached this relatively high entropy position till much later. We expect it to be later than it is. If in the same situation we resign ourselves to the situation and quietly read an enjoyable novel, then our mental disorder is low (small ΔS) and for the same time interval (Δt), the angle θ is relatively small. Our perception is that time has passed quickly because normally we would have reached this entropy position sooner. We expect it to be earlier than it is, but we know it is later as we have read a lot of the novel.

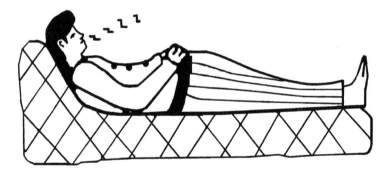

Harry selects the low entropy route.

Whilst reading your novel you observe three businessmen—we will call them Tom, Dick and Harry—who look as if they have been to the convention you noticed advertised in town. The workaholic businessman Tom, with slicked-back hair and striped shirt, gets out his papers, and time also passes quickly for him if he makes calm and steady progress through his work. However, businessman Dick has that worried look of a harassed middle manager and his top shirt button is undone and his tie loosened. Dick has some difficult decisions to make based on some badly prepared reports that he is struggling to understand. It is clear, from the increasing jumble of papers around Dick and his increasing exasperation, that he is making slow progress. Both businessmen are probably consuming more exergy than if they were reading a novel, but then they are both producing some useful work.

Businessman Harry, on the other hand, is bored. He is laid-back, literally. His jacket is laid over the seat next to him, his tie on top of it, and he relaxes. He stares moronically into the middle distance of the airport lounge and he dozes. Harry creates very little entropy—he is succeeding in controlling his entropy vector very tightly—but he has not done any work.

In our modern business environment with our in-trays constantly filling, Harry has fallen behind the other two, and if he continues in the same style his business will fail or he will be fired, or both! Of course, if his doze leaves him refreshed and he polishes off his work on the connecting flight, all will be well, but at the moment his entropy vector has an angle below the natural level defined by the working habits of his contemporaries. Dick is less effective than Tom because his vector angle is high and significantly above the natural level, so that exergy is wasted on entropy creation. Businessman Tom is the most effective. Whilst he is creating some disorder it is minimised and, because he is efficient, he is getting and keeping ahead of the game in terms of useful work done.

Of course, time is running at the same rate for you and all three businessmen. The perceptions are different and the useful work done is different. If you read your novel, then have a sleep for an hour, wake up and eat a chocolate bar before settling down to do some work, time would appear to speed up and slow down like the shadow of the aeroplane. For optimum effectiveness, we need to keep our entropy vector under control.

Dick made little progress because the meaning of the reports was hard to grasp and because the decisions were difficult. A key factor in reducing disorder is the clear and concise transmission of information. Well-written, lucid reports containing the key information without waffle and embellishment would have helped him to be more effective. They would be quicker to read and understand. This would increase confidence and hence reduce the stress levels associated with decision-making. This would save time and reduce disorder arising both from wrong decisions and anxiety over decision-making.

Did we just say 'This would save time'? Sadly, it will not. Business people glibly say that time is money, but it is not. There are no banks or building societies that accept deposits of time. Instead, time flies on, like our aeroplane. What does seem to be true is that how you spend your time is at least as important as how you spend your money. In our story, the appropriate use of time in the preparation of a report would have enabled decision-making to occur more quickly and thus made an element of time available for other tasks or for relaxation. Dick, like everyone else, deserves a break now and again. Efficient report writing, efficient decision-making and a bit of a break give an optimum, composite entropy vector. All the necessary work is done, time has passed quickly and Dick will be neither stressed nor bored.

Information and knowledge

We touched above on the relationship between time management, information management and effective (i.e. low entropy) work. Information management is a major subject and worthy of some consideration. Nowadays, most of us have access to what is effectively an infinite quantity of information. However, in order to use the information we need to convert it into knowledge.

Knowledge implies assimilation of the information in an ordered fashion, which allows us to understand and interpret beyond the limit of the bare facts provided as information. Of course, this assimilation process requires both time and the expenditure of exergy but, as with Dick and his reports, this can be time well spent and can provide the makings of an effective entropy vector. When we have knowledge of a topic, we can operate more effectively within the topic area. Daimler Chrysler must acknowledge this, because they have a 'knowledge management' approach whilst most organisations only have an information technology (IT) approach and leave their staff to struggle to convert information into knowledge.

The danger is that the knowledge portfolio of an organisation constantly degrades as people leave for other jobs or as they retire. In business, we must educate our staff to appropriate levels so that they can deal with the situations presented to them. We must also present information to them in a way that it is easily and rapidly assimilated and understood. This usually means presenting concise and precise information. It includes keeping verbosity to a minimum level that is compatible with easy comprehension.

Protection against extraneous or irrelevant material is also important. This may arise from our own information flows and formats, and we should be able to rectify this intrusion. Another common source is distractions that are external to the task in hand. These may vary from the talk radio on the factory floor to too many visitors in the open plan office. We need to provide an environment in which staff can focus sufficient concentration on the job. In the work environment, the sources of distraction should be very much under our control, though if the task does not sufficiently stimulate staff then the distraction might be thought to be beneficial. A high degree of delicacy may be required to minimise the temporary increase in disorder caused by upset staff who take exception to your removal of what they see as desirable.

The real solution is to provide more stimulating tasks, since energy is being wasted on distraction. It will probably be advantageous to automate the boring, repetitive task using modern technology. In higher wage economies this is increasingly the cost-driven solution too. It is, of course, fair to say that there is some evidence that background music can calm people, thus making them better able to cope with stressful situations. There is a trade-off between efficiency losses due to distraction and those due to stress. The entropy vector is relentless, there is no escape, but there are choices; the music played by surgeons during major operations contrasts sharply with the muzak played in shopping malls.

We have noted that Dick made slow progress because the reports he was working on were badly prepared. The second reason that Dick made slow progress was associated with the difficult decisions he needed to make. Difficult decisions are unavoidable at some time or other. Often they are difficult because we have inadequate information upon which to base them; so knowledge is an important factor again. Also, some people are able to take decisions easily and this kind of temperament is well suited to those jobs where any decision is better than none. Decision-making skills can be taught and developed in anyone, the extent depending on natural aptitude and the quality of the training, but it is significantly enhanced by support from superiors. Effective delegation and support of subordinates allows an organisation to run smoothly and in an orderly manner.

However, there is another issue here and one with a time dimension. Shuffling of the decisions to be made into a logical sequence can lower the stress levels associated with making the decisions. This means that decisions should naturally follow one after the other and the spacing between them can be stretched to allow optimum time for gathering and ordering information before taking the decision. This stretches the horizontal axis of the vector, decreasing the vector angle. It might also reduce the disorder created by a decision, thus further reducing the angle. Of course, 'pacing the decisions' can be taken too far and, in the extreme, failing to make a decision gives a vector angle below the natural vector, leading to instability as events overtake the business.

To summarise, we can improve our effectiveness by controlling our entropy vector and this in turn affects our perception of time. We argued that time spent in preparing information in a clear manner enables easier, faster and better decision-making. We also suggested that the removal of distractions could help to minimise wasted time. Thirdly, we proposed that by providing and supporting an unambiguous structure for delegation we could cut out delays and, finally, by arranging decisions into a logical time sequence, we give ourselves the chance of making better and easier decisions. In all cases, we will have put effort into reducing the entropy by creating some order or by reducing the disorder. All of our actions are likely to have required us to use time in preparation where others may have 'saved time'. Their 'savings' are illusions and, overall, we will have achieved more tasks, more usefully and more effectively. We can also expect to have lowered stress levels, both of ourselves and of our colleagues, which will allow us all to continue to make maximum use of our time.

The march of time

Having enjoyed the idea of time being like an aeroplane in the sky, let us now see it as an infantry battalion on the march. Time can be considered as a resource and, as individuals, we have a finite amount of time allotted to us. In our analogy, we have a fixed number of troops with a finite amount of energy and supplies. We can use them productively and we can also fritter them away. In this sense our battalion, time, is no different from exergy. It is another form of work potential. We can organise our lives to use time more effectively but the act of organisation consumes time. This is equivalent to consuming exergy to create a local pocket of order and low entropy, and it is clearly better to prevent disorder taking control since otherwise considerable time will then have to be spent overcoming the disorder. In a business, we have a finite amount of time available and time management becomes a major issue. If we can do things faster than our competitors, then there is usually a commercial benefit to be gained. If we do things slower, then there is much to be lost! The following example shows the size of the problem. There are some underlying assumptions and the figures are approximate. We will skip the detail and give only the results of the calculation.

In a fast-growing marketplace (say, 20% market growth), with severe price pressure (say, 12% annual price erosion) and a limited product life expectancy (say, 5 years), a delay of 6 months in launching your product can cost you a third of after-tax profits. Let's put that another way: you would make half as much again if you had launched the product on time.

Of course, we need to keep costs down, at least to the level of our competition, and in the above example, production costs of around 10% above the budgeted level result in the loss of 20% of potential after-tax profits.

Customers are prepared to pay for speed of service but speed has a limited value. A shorter time equates to a smaller horizontal component (Δt) of the entropy vector, giving a larger vector angle, θ, on the assumption that the disorder created by the service is the same irrespective of the speed of service. But we know that large vector angles are associated with inefficiency, so the angle must not be allowed to get too big. Entropy creation must be kept under tight control to limit the vertical component (ΔS) of the vector, and controlling entropy costs exergy and in business terms this usually means money. Conversely, customers like low costs, but if we achieve this by being slower than the marketplace, then our business is likely to fail. Customers may well want a cheap service but not if it costs them convenience. An example of this situation is the Transatlantic passenger service. A limited number of customers paid to fly by Concorde, just sufficient to make it economic, at least when the development costs were ignored. Almost no one is prepared to go by ocean liner these days, because it is slow and, as a consequence, the scheduled service has disappeared.

The cost of providing a service can be defined in terms of the exergy or the available resources used. In turn this is closely related to the amount

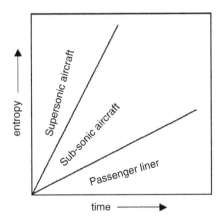

of entropy created, because a proportion of the exergy will always be lost in creation of entropy. Hence, if we can minimise entropy creation we can make a significant contribution to reducing costs. Engineers know that a reversible process is more closely approached when changes are incremental. This implies that a process should proceed very slowly in order to minimise entropy creation. Hence fast processes are always going to involve more losses than slower ones. This is why faster cars cost more to run than slow ones. But if this is true, why then does a 36-year-old bottle of whisky cost more than a 12-year-old bottle? Once the distillery has reached a steady state, the production of 36-year-old bottles is the same as for the 12-year-old bottle. Of course, the reason lies in the capital investment associated with laying down the bottles for 36 years rather 12 years. Entropic degradation ensures erosion of the capital tied up in the maturing whisky and the distillery wants to make up for that loss.

Only a few products can command higher prices for slower production times. In a business we must seek a balance between incremental processes that tend to be highly efficient but provide products too similar to the competition to enable high prices (and high profits) and fast processes, where highly differentiated products may be produced but at production costs that require higher prices (and/or larger volumes) than the market can tolerate in order to give the desire profit margin. In terms of exergy or assets, slow processes are less wasteful but entropic degradation erodes the tied-up assets, whereas fast processes waste assets but there is less time for degradation. A mathematician would happily take these statements, assign some symbols to the degradation rate, the wastage rates, and prices, manipulate some algebra and provide us with an equation defining the optimum rate of production.

Solving such an equation is not so simple. For instance, we do not know the entropic degradation rate, so we cannot precisely calculate the optimum production rate. So, no simple answers; no chance to 'paint by numbers'—that would be too easy and entropy itself will ensure that nothing is that easy!

However, there are some guidelines that can assist our thinking. We have to watch our competitors and our own balance sheet. If we treat money as the principal asset, then the entropic degradation rate is controlled by the global economy, and this will mean that the price you get for your goods is determined by your competitors in your marketplace, with that marketplace itself ruled by international factors. You will not compete favourably on products with a high labour content if those products can be made to an equivalent quality in low-labour-rate economies. Neither will you compete successfully in export markets if there is a sudden swing in exchange rates that makes your goods more expensive (or your profit vanishingly small). For comfort, a company needs to perform just ahead of the 'average' competitor who defines, in that market, the natural entropy vector. If a company finds itself falling behind the natural vector, it can speed up production, thus shortening the horizontal (time) axis of the vector and increasing the angle. A steeper angle, in principle, will take the company back to its comfort position, just above the natural entropy vector. However, a steep curve means a high entropy course and the company will need to monitor the production costs and watch out for sources of entropy such as the wasted effort on the factory or office floor, or stress levels in our workforce or increased pollution levels. All of these are potential sources of future trouble and can prevent a successful move to the comfort zone.

Recoveries can and do work but it is unlikely that the recovered company will regain a former position of dominance. One could point to IBM, which has made great strides in the last decade to reposition itself, and could speculate that Marks and Spencer will emerge from current difficulties and reposition itself. Successful repositioning is possible; reinstatement is rare. Time has moved on; entropy has increased; there is no going back.

The smart advice is that it is better not to slip behind the competition in the first place and an alternative way of staying ahead is to make innovative products. This is discussed in Chapter 8, 'Creativity and Innovation'.

No more time

Well, broadly we hope that this is not true, but this chapter is coming to an end and there is time only to summarise. We began by looking at the quantum-mechanical explanation of the universe and faced the concept of time travelling both forwards and backwards. We found comfort in the idea of arrows that indicated the direction of time and found them all to be related to entropy in one way or another.

We recapped on what we mean by the entropy vector and asked how the management of our entropy vector might affect our perception of time. Our conclusion was that time can appear to travel at various speeds. We likened it to watching the shadow of an aeroplane on a hillside. The aeroplane moves steadily but the shadow does not. We also noted that if we can perceive time to be passing quickly and usefully we have the makings of an effective workplace. We met Tom, Dick and Harry and considered a variety of ways to control entropy and thereby improve our time management and stress levels.

Finally, we looked at the way time itself affects the horizontal component of our entropy vector. It is a resource, like exergy, and needs to be used in such a way as to give an entropy vector that provides us with advantage.

Notes and quotes

- *A Brief History of Time—From the Big Bang to Black Holes*, by S.W. Hawking (Bantam, London, 1988).
- R. Dawkins, *The Blind Watchmaker*. We should acknowledge that the idea of using a grandfather clock to explain the workings of the universe may have been influenced by Dawkins' suggestion that there is (or is not) a blind watchmaker somewhere in the background.
- Factors affecting lifetime profit? The details given in the 'March of Time' section are from a paper presented by Colin Mynott in a 1997 series of Business Link seminars, entitled 'Successful Product Development'.
- For more on decisions, see *Making Management Decisions*, 2nd edition, by Steve Cooke and Nigel Slack (Prentice-Hall, Englewood Cliffs, 1991).
- For those interested in time symmetry physics and/or asymmetric universes, we recommend *Time's Arrow and Archimedes' Point*, by Huw Price (Oxford University Press, 1996).

7

Managing Disorder

*good management techniques • teams and training • flat-lining •
control freaks • pantomimes and orchestras • change and risk*

'Just hold this, don't touch that ... aarrghh, too late!' We have all experienced the descent into chaos of a group of people who are supposed to be
working together but are actually each doing their own thing. Everyone
might start by heading in the same direction or at least with the same
objective in mind but, as each person does what they think is best,
progress towards the objective can become painfully slow. Once the
entropy vector is taken into account, it should not be very surprising that
a group activity tends towards disorder and ineffectiveness.

The second law of thermodynamics tells us that entropy tends to
increase to a maximum. The entropy of a group will tend to increase
unless something is done to stop it. Increasing disorder and a lack of
co-ordination in a group activity is a perfectly natural state of events. So,
what can be done to make a group more effective? What can a manager
do to keep entropy under control, and is this always a good thing? All of
us are managing in disorder, for there is always plenty of disorder around.

Maybe there are techniques and approaches that allow us to manage
disorder—or at least to limit how much we create. In this chapter, we
shall look at some of the characteristics of teams and management and
investigate how differing management styles and techniques shape the
entropy vector.

People are not atoms

It is true, in the extreme, that people are made up of atoms (mostly carbon, hydrogen and oxygen), but they are more than sacks of chemicals. People can change their behaviour. Every interaction is unique. Group dynamics are unpredictable. Individuals can be driven by their own sense of importance or expectation or desire. No obvious external force is required.

Given these differences, is it tenable to suggest that a law of nature (the second law of thermodynamics, to be precise) applies outside the scientific boundary of heat engines? We argue that it is: that entropy is a measure of efficiency in all processes and that heat engines are simply one example of a process. In detail, our arguments may be loose at the edges and purists may shudder. We are not so naïve as to expect a perfect mapping from science to business but the underlying themes hold good. There is no doubt either that the language maps across. We talk in business often enough about energy and disorder, and one final example of language merits attention. Our thermodynamicist colleague, Robin, will patiently explain that in a defined system, the only way to achieve a decrease in entropy is by cooling. Our entrepreneurial colleague, Anthony, refers us to the first MBA lecture he gave, on the subject of better (i.e. less inefficient, less disorganised) management. It was entitled 'Facts in Place of Emotion: Cool It'.

Potential = Collaboration + Training

Clearly, things improve in group work when there is collaboration between the members. This can be provided by leadership or management and also occurs when the individual members of the group have knowledge appropriate to the task. Both training and management constrain the freedom of individuals, lowering the entropy of the group and increasing its work potential. Normal management constraints are likely to make a group more effective in tackling routine or predictable tasks; but too much constraint will inhibit its performance in situations where creativity is needed. In general, management is required to achieve a fine balance, for individuals normally resent too much constraint of freedom. Plato may have suggested that 'slavery is perfect freedom' but most of us do not see it that way. There are, however, some areas that more than others give us an indication of 'low entropy' management.

The army, in particular, is very good at lowering entropy and creating teams. Infantry soldiers are drilled day after day to respond to a series of commands. In battle a soldier will face horrific sights and it is crucial to his safety and those of his comrades that he should respond to commands in a totally predictable manner. The entropy of a platoon of soldiers is very low because they are highly constrained and ordered by discipline and have a good knowledge of the operations they will be asked to carry out.

A production line is another example of a low entropy system. The workers are highly constrained by both their training and the equipment they operate. The result is a very efficient system for manufacturing a particular product. Low entropy systems such as the production line or the army platoon are excellent for dealing with repetitive or predictable tasks, but poor systems for responding to new requirements. A great deal of effort is required to convert a production line from making tractors to one producing soap powder, or to persuade the platoon to write and perform an opera!

If free to do so, individuals in a group will act under their own initiative. If everyone uses their initiative in an uncoordinated way, then the outcome is unpredictable. The single, desired outcome is less probable than one of the many undesired outcomes. If they are motivated, guided or trained to collaborate, a more desirable outcome is likely. A lack of collaboration can be equated with entropy; the better the collaboration, the less entropy generated. As we know from our earlier skirmish with the army platoon, knowledge or information is the other key factor in the success of a team; without it, success is unlikely. Without a map even the best-organised orienteering team is unlikely to win the race. By increasing the knowledge of a team we can lower its entropy and increase its exergy or work potential. We saw in Chapter 3 that information is negative entropy, and knowledge is used here rather than information to indicate information that has been absorbed and understood by the team. This is an important and practical extension of the concept of information.

For example, along with millions of others you might have a copy of the *Oxford English Dictionary* sitting on your book-shelf. As a consequence, you have access to the information on the etymological origins of millions of words in the English language, but the information is of little use until you study the book and acquire the information as knowledge. Knowledge lowers the entropy of individuals and teams, thus enhancing their work potential. The tendency of entropy to increase ensures that knowledge will be lost or forgotten.

Thomas Stewart, in his book *Intellectual Capital: The New Wealth of Organisations*, reminds us that companies need to convert the knowledge and know-how of individuals and work practices into written form (structural capital, in his terminology) so that it is available for others in the organisation to use. They need to do this not just to stop themselves slipping behind their competitors but also because this approach, more than any other, puts the company in the best position to move forwards and derive greater value from what they have.

To recap, in the context of managing teams, the exergy or work potential is the sum of the collaboration and knowledge possessed by the team. Collaboration is non-specific whereas knowledge is task-specific. This explains why the well-trained platoon will struggle to write and perform the opera. They are high on collaboration but low on knowledge about opera. The creation of a highly trained team involves a great of deal of work and use of resources—that is obvious and well known from our experience of life. It also follows from the second law of thermodynamics, because the creation of a local pocket of low entropy requires the expenditure of exergy or available resources. The total change of entropy on a global scale must be positive. We can only create a local reduction in entropy by using up some exergy, and the entropy resulting elsewhere from this use will outweigh the reduction we have obtained. Sad but true.

What is less obvious and often forgotten is that to maintain the effectiveness of the team, a continuing use of exergy is required, typically in the form of training. Why does the team inevitably need ongoing training? It is because of the tendency of entropy to increase, thus gradually destroying the well-ordered team. We can see this in a number of ways. Personality clashes and jealousies can erode collaboration. Knowledge is forgotten or goes out of date. Sloppy execution of tasks results from idleness or lack of practice. And, of course, human nature plays a part. Most people do not have a predisposition towards a disciplined, regulated approach to life and so they will progressively drift away from the way they were trained to do something.

Managing the entropy vector

Team leaders or managers are a crucial part of any team and their key role is to harness the entropy vector so that it is used to the advantage of their team. When the platoon leader is relatively unconstrained in his or her thinking, then the highly trained soldiers have far greater potential than if they are led by an automaton. This is because a well-disciplined workforce that follows precisely the commands of an innovative leader is able to tackle unfamiliar tasks.

Similarly, a good production manager can behave creatively to meet exceptional demands. However, these two examples are rather special cases, because huge amounts of energy are invested in producing the constrained teams and the payback for that investment is greatest when the team carries out the tasks for which it has been trained. Management will want the production line to operate as designed, producing widgets cheaply and quickly so that the cost of creating the constraints can be recovered as quickly as possible. The taxpayer, who is prepared to pay a high price for security, pays the cost for the army and will want it to perform correctly.

The natural, unremitting increase in entropy guarantees that change will occur. Organisations must be able to respond to these changes if they are to survive. One way of responding is to retrain the team, but this is expensive and in a rapidly changing environment may not be viable. A team or organisation needs to respond effectively and rapidly to changes in its circumstances, and to be able to do this, its manager must raise its entropy by removing constraints. The entropy vector needs to be in the positive direction but difficulties occur when the entropy gets too high, for then the team will become disordered and ineffective.

It is the role of a manager to control the entropy vector and ensure that the level of entropy is correct for the circumstances. The objective is to have an internal entropy vector appropriate to the natural entropy vector of the environment but we cannot measure either vector in absolute terms. Since the natural vector is governed by the environment or market in which your business is operating, it pays to have good external links to help judge the rate and type of change. Such links include connections with customers, suppliers, intermediaries, professionals, trade associations, universities.

It also depends on the industry you are in. For example, if you are manufacturing spoons, then the market does not change very rapidly, so that the natural entropy vector indicates only a small increase in entropy with time. Consequently, your company vector should be similar but with a rate of change just ahead of your competitors.

If your company is still making spoons by hand in the little workshop built by your great-grandfather and using his tools and techniques, then it is probably about to become insolvent. Your entropy vector is too close to being flat or at zero and the industry has moved (albeit slowly) towards mass-production methods, which enable your competitors to make products of comparable quality much more cheaply.

We are probably familiar with the expression 'flat-lining' from US medical dramas, indicating an absence of heartbeat in an unfortunate patient. Entropy flat-lining is a similarly critical condition in organisations.

But back to our spoon company, and if the managing director realises that he is 'flat-lining' during his government-sponsored trade mission to Korea and returns home to change the factory overnight, the result is also likely to be disaster. The entropy vector will be too steep. Clearly, making changes of this order of magnitude requires research, planning and consultation with staff, suppliers and major customers. Training of personnel at all levels from top to bottom is needed, otherwise the new technology will fail to realise its full potential. All of this requires time and so lowers the gradient of the entropy vector, thus increasing the probability of success.

As any managing director will tell you, there are many ways to fail but only a very few ways to ensure success. Put another way, success is the less probable outcome and hence requires the expenditure of more exergy than failure.

Management types

All managers use up energy in their jobs but the way in which they utilise the exergy has a profound effect on the success of their organisations. If exergy is dissipated in wasteful, unproductive activity, then a lot of entropy will be generated without much useful work. So, we can divide managers into four categories:

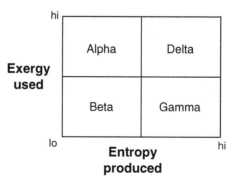

Alpha managers are the most desirable, because they consume a large amount of exergy or work potential and generate little entropy, so this implies that a lot of exergy has been converted into useful work. On the other hand, in most circumstances delta managers are to be avoided, because they use a lot of work potential but most of it is lost in unproductive activity. Gamma managers are almost as bad but they are less active, so that less is wasted. The beta manager is a fairly neutral character, because although the entropy generation is low, the exergy consumption is low too, so not much is happening at all. Once again the probability of having successful managers seems to be low—25% if managers are distributed evenly across the four categories. This is the second law at work again: *You can't have it just anyway you like.*

Our entropy–exergy matrix in this context is not dissimilar to the leadership grid matrix proposed by Robert Blake. There, 'Concern for People' is plotted against 'Concern for Production'. Carrying out simple mapping, where we equate high people concern with high exergy used and high production concern with low entropy production, we readily see that alpha managers are in the desirable quadrant.

Of course, real life situations are more complicated since managers can use exergy to build constraints and structures into the workplace. The pioneering study at Ohio State University in the middle of the last century looked at concern for people against supervisory structures—in other words, the division of exergy used between supporting staff directly and seeking to establish frameworks within which the staff should operate. Poor structures and low concern for staff gave, not surprisingly, the worst production levels. A mix of high and low gave middling production figures, with by far the better results arising where the structures were better-established. Highly structured environments matched with high concern for staff gave the highest production levels.

At first glance, these results indicate that highly structured organisations can produce both happy and unhappy workers, with the former being more productive. Does this mean that productivity is independent of structure and that highly constrained systems work best? We suggest not and would argue that, once again, the entropy vector is at work. The critical feature is how the exergy is used and what balance of disorder is created. Rigid, highly directive leaders who apply rigid directive structures leave no responsibility or trust with the team, which becomes uncooperative. Disorder and dissatisfaction spread as a malaise. On the other hand, managers who exhibit consideration for and trust in their subordinates create management structures in which responsibility is delegated and information is disseminated, so that workers become empowered and the potential of the team is enhanced. With the right people management, structures that allow freedom (and hence disorder) result in less wasteful (i.e. lower-entropy production) than poor people concern and tightly organised work environments, despite the initial expectation that tight organisations will give minimum disorder.

So, how do you spot these different types? And, how you do become an alpha manager?

Delta managers are energetic, using large quantities of exergy but wasting it. So, this type of manager will be darting here, there and everywhere interfering in everything and expressing an opinion on every minor detail. Delta managers are good at issuing commands but also countermands, which waste the efforts of their team. They do not allow their staff to do anything on their own, which inhibits and de-motivates the staff, so that they become inefficient. Energy is wasted in complaining about the boss.

No clear leadership is provided and so the collaboration within the team is lowered, increasing its disorder or entropy. The team is ineffective and delta managers spend their time rushing from one crisis to another because they do not trust their staff to deal with them. This is a self-fulfilling prophecy, because the staff do not attempt to deal with the crisis in the knowledge that the boss will be along in a moment to take over. With some managers this is probably the only knowledge that they impart to their staff. So, the knowledge level of the team is also low, which further reduces the work potential.

Gamma managers are similar to delta managers but significantly less energetic. This results in less consumption of exergy, but the proportion lost to entropy is high, just as with the delta managers. They may not rush around and have as much of a physical presence as delta managers but their 'presence' is always felt, if unseen, and staff delay and defer action 'knowing' it would be wrong. You may think of the expression 'gamma' in terms of gamma radiation—dangerous (but there is worse), invisible and all-pervasive. Gamma and delta managers could be described as 'control freaks', because they do not delegate and hence much of the work potential in their staff is lost. Control freaks, you may have noticed, are not effectively in control of their team or the situation; instead, chaos and disorder reigns. 'Freak' is usually understood to mean 'monster' but perhaps one of the alternative meanings of the word more appropriately describes the behaviour of this type of manager—'a sudden causeless change or turn of mind'. Team members feel undervalued and alienated by the retention of all responsibility by the manager and so collaboration within the team begins to break down. Control freaks tend to prevent dissemination of knowledge' so the entropy of the team is increased further.

The delta manager usually fails to achieve the necessary understanding before he or she acts. The delta manager's actions might be well-intentioned but the lack of consultation and delegation ultimately increases the disorder.

Gamma managers are less energetic in their stifling of staff, but operate by tending to block the decisions of subordinates by not responding when a decision is required of them and by not informing their team when a decision has been made. All of these tactics waste exergy but tend to wreak less havoc than the frenetic activity of a delta manager.

When gamma managers are in charge, the entropy vector assumes something close to its natural orientation (though on the disordered rather than ordered side because of their interventions) and disorder increases until the organisation becomes inefficient and ineffective. With delta managers, there is considerably more unhelpful intervention and the rate of increase of disorder is higher though the destination is the same.

Of course, other factors are involved and the time taken to descend into disorder through entropic degradation will also depend on the degree of training that the team already possesses and the rate at which the environment is changing. An untrained team will become disordered almost immediately, whereas a well-trained one will function effectively for some time and its performance will only disintegrate gradually. A gamma or delta manager can look quite good if he takes over a team previously led by an alpha. When circumstances or the environment changes rapidly, the effect of the gamma and delta managers will be very quickly apparent.

It has become fashionable to refer to narcissistic leaders whose vision is for themselves rather than for the organisation, and whose actions are driven by their own aggrandisement rather the greater good of the team. Delta managers are likely to fall prey to this failing, whereas it is impossible to be an alpha manager and a narcissist since alpha managers need to empower their teams and share the glory with them.

Alpha managers consumes exergy at a terrific rate but with very productive results. They could be described as 'energising managers' and, like delta managers, can be seen rushing around. However, with alpha managers, this is usually because their enthusiasm results in their taking on too many simultaneous activities and having too few subordinates for effective delegation. Alpha managers are alpha-grade: first-rate, gold-star, top-of-the-form. These people are good at delegating responsibility and supporting the decisions made by their subordinates. They give their staff the freedom and confidence to show their own initiative within clear guidelines; guidelines which curtail individual initiative to some extent, thus increasing the potential for collaboration within the team. Tight guidelines are required to maximise work potential, but loose guidelines are needed to allow creativity to deal with new circumstances.

The alpha manager is good at judging this balance. He or she is also enthusiastic and this is infectious, which engenders team spirit and increases the collaboration and work potential of the team. This type of person flourishes on increased exergy generated through increased responsibility. The increased exergy could be internal and personal, in the form of initiative; or external, in the form of resources (people, equipment, funding) made available by the company.

The less energetic version of an alpha manager is the beta manager. If one can excuse the pun, beta managers can get betta; they can improve because they already have the ability to manage without generating a lot of entropy. They need to set themselves harder targets (which may involve promotion and may be psychologically difficult if there is no chance of promotion and they are content with their current duties, status and pay). Beta managers delegate effectively and provide leadership but are more laid-back in their own approach. This means that the team is likely to be less dynamic, so that the productive work generated is less simply because less exergy is being consumed. This can be advantageous for leaders of research-and-development teams, but is not appropriate for production lines with high capital costs where a return on the investment is required on a reasonable timescale.

Of course, the classification of managers is not as black-and-white as it has been painted in the preceding paragraphs. People do not divide neatly into high and low exergy categories. In reality people fall somewhere between these distinct types and possess characteristics that aren't just to do with exergy and entropy.

Raymond Meredith Belbin, more than most, gets to grips with what makes a team tick and why one team achieves so much more than another. Whilst individuals do not fit exactly into neat classifications of personality type, he found that certain characteristics predominate in individuals and the natural (or 'under stress') tendency is in one direction rather than another. Thus, a large organisation needs a mix of different types of people; indeed, the right different sorts of people to perform well, or, in the language of this book, to control the entropy vector. Belbin shows that this is important within teams. 'Teams,' he says, 'are a question of balance. What is needed is not well-balanced individuals, but individuals who balance well with one another.'

It is equally important at team leadership level. A surplus of managers of one particular type does not provide the diversity needed to cope with the variety of circumstances that an organisation will face. Too many gamma and delta managers simply multiplies the disadvantages already discussed. Too many relaxed beta managers could lead to a dearth of strategic thinking and competitors will steal the lead from you. Most organisations do not have the space for too many energising alpha managers who can easily end up competing with one another and lose sight of the need to compete in a wider environment.

It is clear from our discussions so far that alpha managers are most valuable and so to advance your career you should clearly aim to be an alpha manager. This means you should be able to communicate clearly with your team and to delegate responsibilities unambiguously (which includes standing by decisions made by subordinates). You must be able to provide training for your team so that they will possess both collaboration skills and knowledge sufficient to overcome the circumstances that they are likely to encounter. Finally, you need to be enthusiastic and energetic about the tasks in hand. You may decide that this is a tall order and settle for being a beta manager or something in between!

Fit for the purpose

There are circumstances where creativity is the principal aim and, as described in the next chapter, this requires a distinctly positive entropy vector. If you are unconstrained in your thinking, then you can produce a collection of random, disordered ideas. Many of these ideas will be useless, but amongst them will be the occasional gem that contains the solution to a problem or the potential for innovation. If a group is required to be creative or to brainstorm a particular problem, then it is vital that they are put together without training as a team.

The easier task for the manager is to train the group as a team so that it will respond in known ways to known stimuli. But this will make the group relatively constrained so that it does not have a very positive entropy vector; that is, it will be less creative. The output from the 'untrained' group will tend to be random and so a skilful team leader is required to harness the creativity.

If the aim is to design a new product that will dominate the market place and make a healthy profit for the company, then a group of people will be required with expertise in a number of areas such as design, production engineering, marketing and finance. The knowledge level of the group is high but the collaboration level can be very low. Each of these experts will need to be imaginative, creative and free-thinking. The diversity of the education and background of the group is as important as their individual ability to be creative, but the management of this diversity also adds to the skills required from the leader. These skills must include generating an environment in which individuals feel uninhibited about expressing new and perhaps controversial ideas, guiding the discussions towards the new design of products without stifling the flow of creative thinking, and sifting the useful ideas from the random output. These skills are much more likely to be present in the alpha manager described above than in the others.

In passing, we can see from the above analysis why an organisational matrix structure is so good for new projects and product developments and why the management of a matrix is such a hard task.

Of course, there are occasions when training the group as a team is important. If we are listening to a concert we want the horns to be in sympathy with the violins and we certainly do not want a jazz solo from the clarinets in the middle of a Bach pastoral. On the other hand, if we were watching a pantomime, we would look forward with relish to the occasional ad lib.

Talk of orchestras leads neatly to Benjamin Zander, conductor of the Boston Symphony Orchestra and someone who has an increasing international reputation as a speaker on management. One of his themes is the manager as a conductor, and the metaphor is interesting:

Leadership and teamwork together can produce exceptional performances.

- A conductor has to do everything before it happens—doing it at the time is too late.
- A conductor needs to have a 'listening'—the orchestra must trust him, and the audience must be enrolled.
- A conductor must trust the orchestra, empower them. After all, they play the music, he doesn't.
- The good conductor has a vision of distinction. He creates great music from what otherwise would simply be a good song.

A good conductor strips away unwanted material and lets the music through; he does not get in the way. With a high quality team, such an approach is to be recommended, but what if the team at your disposal is rather more like some earnest but under-trained amateurs preparing for a pantomime than the city's premier orchestra? We should also consider the pantomime stage manager as a metaphor for a manager:

- A stage manager knows that poor support detail can destroy the whole programme.
- A stage manager organises the links; they are as important as the events.
- A stage manager creates the environment for the prima donnas to perform.

- A stage manager chooses the special effects carefully and makes them count.
- A stage manager is unseen and unnoticed, unless things go wrong.

We can also characterise team members in the same way as their leaders, so that high exergy, low entropy members are top performers and high exergy, high entropy members are keen beginners. If we substitute commitment for exergy and incompetence for entropy, then we arrive at the development levels suggested by Paul Hershey and Kenneth Blanchard.

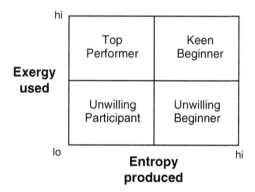

Different situations require different management skills. The more disorganised world of the amateur pantomime—the high entropy environment—needs a manager who can reduce the disorder, whereas the concert orchestra—the low entropy environment—needs a manager who can minimise disorder occurring.

In a business context, we can look a little more broadly at this—or at least it is possible, as some management recruitment consultants will inevitably do, to develop another two-by-two matrix. The matrix will go something like this. On the y-axis we plot the size of step change, and on the x-axis, the size of the time interval involved.

An environment such as the bottom-left-hand box requires only very small changes and very small planning intervals. This is the easiest management job. Even the delta manager has difficulty in generating too much disorder here. Go right along the bottom of the grid and the task is small changes but in the context of a long planning period. The manager is required to build steadily and competently. Beta leaders can operate very successfully in the bottom right corner, bringing about transactional change using known solutions and techniques and incremental innovation. A gamma manager would get by but the end point would be substantially less valuable with him in charge.

Go up from the bottom-left-hand box to the situation where fairly large change is required in a short period of time. This is crisis management. Given a big enough crisis, a delta manager can operate here for quite some time before being found out. Indeed, since some of his actions may, by chance, be the right ones and since many crises are in part solved by changes in the environment and events out of the control of the manager, the luckier delta managers may end up being congratulated (and, heaven forbid, promoted).

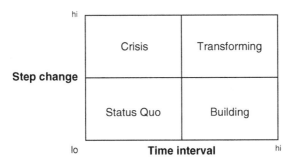

Only alpha managers or transformational leaders stand any realistic chance of success in the top-right-hand corner, where substantial, radical and creative change is required in the context of a sensibly long planning period.

Education, efficiency and economies

In the modern world, in which technology is increasingly dominating everything that we do, education is a major factor in the performance of both individuals and organisations. It is not possible to put together a team of unconstrained thinkers, because we are all constrained by the education that we have received and we need an educated team to ensure that we have the capacity for knowledge. However, there are some degrees of freedom available. The engineer in the team will tend to think about a problem in a different way to the accountant.

This is reminiscent of a staff–student cricket match many years ago. We won the toss and decided to bat. The engineers were thinking about process efficiency—who bats first and how to mix up our left- and right-handers. On the other hand, the professor of accounting was on a different plane. 'Who,' he asked, 'has a pencil? We need a pencil to keep score. If we cannot score, there is no point in playing.'

There are also differences at a national level resulting from different cultural approaches. For example, the European higher education system tends to create engineering graduates who are creative and inventive, whereas the tiger economies of Southeast Asia tend to produce graduates who are more formulaic in their approach. It is interesting to relate this to the performance of engineering in the economies. The car, the computer and the television (to name a few products) were invented in Europe, but the tiger economies have made mega-bucks by mass-producing them. The events of the late 1990s suggest that the bankers and financiers in the tiger economies are less formulaic. Their creativity led them into irregular practices and the regulatory system failed to constrain them so that they had an entropy vector that was too positive. The result has been disorder and near-collapse of the economies.

Entropy can only be reduced in local pockets, and there is always a compensatory increase elsewhere. The magnitude of the global increase is always larger than the local reduction. Directors of organisations are apt to refer to the improvements in efficiency they have brought about in their unit but tend to ignore the consequences of the global increase in entropy. These consequences might be unwanted by-products that are often regarded as pollution, or they could be increased stress levels amongst employees. A production manager might believe that something can be gained for nothing by increasing the speed of the production line or the workload per individual, but the cost is probably being paid through increased stress levels experienced by workers. If the speed increase is small the production manager may not appreciate this cost, because the workers may absorb it without complaint or reaction at work, although their families might detect it at home. However, if the increase in speed is larger, the increase in stress will lead to more frequent mistakes and more sickness, both of which have an impact on the organisation. The overall philosophy is called lean manufacturing, but you can have the wrong kind of leanness and anorexia is not advised.

It is not just manufacturing enterprises that tend to neglect the broader consequences of locally lowering the entropy state. In capitalist economies, Thatcherite or Reaganite policies have led to so called 'efficiency savings' in public services such as health and education. These savings involve fewer employees teaching more students, or treating more patients. In financial terms there is a clear gain in efficiency, but the stress levels of the employees rise, which produces a decline in commitment and motivation. The way in which these declines manifest themselves is dependent on the scale of the efficiency savings, the starting point for them, and the management skills of those responsible for their implementation. The concept that something can be gained for nothing simply means that the proponent has ignored or shifted some of the costs and is attempting to violate the first law of thermodynamics: *You can't have something for nothing.*

Ignoring or hiding the costs or consequences has become the preoccupation of 'spin doctors' in our society. These people specialise in portraying a person, organisation or event in the best possible light. The application of the second law of thermodynamics is a good way of seeing through the 'spin'. There must always be a cost or consequence somewhere; it is just a case of looking in the right place, or drawing the boundaries of the system appropriately. *You can't have something for nothing and you can't have it just anyway you like.*

Change and risk

Before we finish, we should take a brief look at the disorder caused by risk taking and the task of a manager to balance the need to take risks with the need to minimise disorder. Managers are fond of talking about risks and rightly so since running a successful organisation involves taking risks. In order to be successful an organisation needs to change and the rate of change that is necessary will depend on the dynamics of the particular environment in which the organisation is operating. Managers and organisations put themselves at risk if their entropy vector falls below the one for their environment. But to keep up competitively involves attempting to predict the changes in the environment. This is a risky business since there is a significant probability that the predictions will be wrong.

As we have already noted, there are more wrong ways to attempt a development than there are right ones. We end up making comments such as 'all other things being equal', which everybody knows really means 'most unlikely'. Managers may pretend that the normal process of entropic degradation will suspend hostilities whilst they try to make some new and risky development. They may even have a precise mathematical calculation to convince themselves that the risk is worth taking, but they are not convincing us! They may have been able to compare various risk options with each other by this calculation but they do not have a measure of the real risk of doing any one of them.

Of course, it is desirable for risk managers to focus on reducing the risks associated with a chosen course of action and to select processes that are less risky than alternatives. This can and should be done. However, the concept of calculating the risks associated with particular processes or actions and using these calculations in the decision making process is flawed.

The quantification of risk is an illusion. The organisation will be over-taken by events driven by the natural positive entropy vector. We would be better off using our precious resources (our dwindling supply of exergy) to leave the risk unquantified and to develop a team capable of operating responsibly and of responding to changing circumstances and a manage-ment structure committed to building collaboration and developing and sharing knowledge. We will return to the question of risk and entropy in a later chapter.

Summary

In this chapter, we have considered managers to have the prime task of managing the entropy vector. We have noted that they can control it by applying procedures and rules and by engendering collaboration in their teams and ensuring that there is good and appropriate information avail-able. We have noted, however, that too little entropy results in the condi-tion of 'flat-lining', where teams and organisations make so few changes that they fall behind peer groups and competitors.

We have not shown a lot of affection for control freaks and spin doctors. Different managers have different styles, and different situations call for different approaches. We would, after all, be disappointed if entropy allowed it to be any other way. There is value in diversity, but not for its own sake. The intelligent and successful manager uses diversity to give the best chance of harnessing the entropy vector to his or her best advantage.

We have worried that the quantification of risk is an illusion and sug-gested that the better use of resources is in building and managing teams capable of responding to change.

Notes and quotes

- *Intellectual Capital*, by Thomas A. Stewart (Nicholas Brealey Publishing, 1998). 'Human capital, the sap flowing beneath the bark of a tree, produces innovation and growth, but that growth ring becomes solid wood, part of the structure of the tree. What leaders need to do is contain and retain knowledge so that it becomes company property. That's structural capital.'
- Liz Fulop, Stephen Linstead and Richard Dunford, in Chapter 6 of *Management: A Critical Text*, edited by L. Fulop and S. Linstead (Macmillan Press, London, 1999), provide a comprehensive and critical

review of leadership theory which covers the ideas proposed by P. Hershey and K. Blanchard (*Management of Organisational Behaviour: Utilising Human Resources* (Prentice-Hall, Englewood Cliffs, NJ, 1996)), and by R. Blake and A.A. McCanse (*Leadership Dilemmas: Grid Solutions* (Gulf, Houston, 1991)).

- Data on the behaviour of managers obtained from assessments by their subordinates was collected in major study at Ohio State University in the 1940s. This has been used extensively in subsequent analyses; see for example: R.M. Stoghill, *Handbook of Leadership* (The Free Press, New York, 1974).

- Raymond Meredith Belbin. 'I believe his work to be the most important single contribution of the past decade to our understanding of how human organisations work and how to make them work better.'— Anthony Jay, in his preface to *Management Teams*, by R. Meredith Belbin (Heinemann, London, 1981).

- 'The Wrong Kind of Lean: Overcommitment and Under-represented Skills on Technology Teams' is the title of an excellent article by William A. Lucas, Edward Shroyer, Brian J. Schwartz and Gerard Noel; Sloan School of Management Working Paper Number 4168 (2000), Massachusetts Institute of Technology.

- The effect of 'over-leanness' on a company's ability to respond to technical change is reviewed by Wesley Cohen and Daniel Levinthal in an article entitled 'Absorptive Capacity', *Administrative Science Quarterly*, 35 (1990), pp. 128–52.

8

Creativity and Innovation

what is creativity? • what is innovation? • harnessing them in business • technology trajectories • woolliness, bananas and knots • entropy and technopy

On the face of it, innovation is easy to define. Surely it is simply the introduction of novelty and new things? Of course, it is harder to do, and we shall come to that in a moment. We shall also find that the definition is a little more complicated too.

As for creativity, well, according to the *Oxford English Dictionary*, it is the process of 'forming out of nothing'. In the context of business or organisations, better definitions include 'invention' and 'ability to bring about something new'. There is a danger of blurring the distinction with innovation—where does the ability to bring about something new end and the introduction of new things begin? Look at it like this. Creativity is the spark that starts the fire; the crack of the gun to start the race; the initiation of a process—called innovation—leading to a new product or a new process, also and confusingly called *the* innovation.

Not every spark leads to a major conflagration. Not every starter's gun initiates a record-breaking race. Similarly with creativity, it can lead to both small and large change (or incremental and radical innovation, if you prefer). Or it may lead to nothing useful at all. No useful work may result from the exergy we apply. Creativity can be a high entropy process.

It is difficult to talk about creativity without referring to the subsequent innovation, but it is worth attention in its own right, for no innovation occurs without the initial creativity.

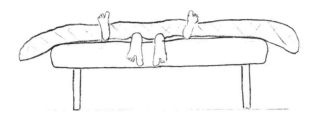

When the spark of an idea meets a nucleus of complementary knowledge.

Three approaches to creativity

In simple terms, there are three approaches to creativity: regurgitation, interpolation and extrapolation.

Regurgitation is the most straightforward and least original, because it consists in applying existing knowledge in a new setting. It is creation for the receiving company but that is all. In the wider world it has been created already. Many creative consultants are simply regurgitating what they have already done. This is fine if the new setting is analogous to the old one but there are hazards. No matter how excellent a manager may have been in a large company, the solutions that worked there may not form the basis of a successful consultancy activity with small firms.

Interpolation involves slightly more originality, because it consists in making sense of existing information in a new way. In science, there is much talk about extending the frontiers of knowledge. Usually this happens in leaps and bounds that leave gaps behind the frontiers. The filling of these gaps could be regarded as interpolative creativity. This should not be regarded as a trivial activity; even relatively small changes—your favourite detergent, now available in a handy pack—can make impressive contributions to annual profits. Sometimes, rather more science is involved.

A recent example of interpolative creativity in the automobile industry is the design, by Mercedes-Benz, of the new generation of small cars. They still have four wheels, two rows of forward-facing seats, and an engine at the front. The creativity is to be found in the strategy for their crashworthiness. The existing design strategy to protect a car's occupants in a head-on collision was centred on energy absorbing structures in front of the engine and structural strength in the passenger compartment to prevent the engine being rammed into it. This approach is viable in a large car but difficult in a small car. In the new generation of small cars, such as the Mercedes A-class, the crashworthiness is designed around the engine being pushed back and under the floor of the passenger compartment rather than into the front of the compartment. This allows comparable energy absorption to be achieved within a much shorter length of car and provides better protection to the occupants. The invention involved here relates to considering existing ideas in new ways. All the pieces are known but the combination and the application are different.

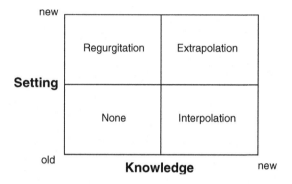

Extrapolation is about extending the frontiers of science, or about escaping from the constraints of current or company thinking. This is the most exciting and difficult of creative activities and is sometimes called 'thinking outside the box'. It can produce the most radical of changes. Take for example the classic story of Henry Ford. One moment Henry was running a little jobbing shop trying to meet customer needs with a choice of engine designs and capacities and various chassis and body-work options. The next, he had the world's first car production line and a standard product in a standard colour. So what were the creative, 'out of the box' ideas? There were two. First, he identified the real and profitable demand that was obscured by the immediate customer request. In other words, to satisfy customer demand by giving the many the essence of what they want (personal, motorised transport) at a price they can afford rather than trying to satisfy the few by individual and attractive designs at individual and unattractive prices. Secondly, the idea to break down the craftsman's job of making a car into discrete activities and make an assembly line that repeatedly and reproducibly gave a highly complicated, 'craftsman' product.

Innovative footsteps

Having introduced creativity and categorised it, perhaps it would be useful at this point to look in more detail at innovation. As we have said, at one level, innovation is simple to define; it is the introduction of novelty or new things. Closer inspection, and certainly reference to the literature, reveal that it is rather more complicated. Various contributors to the literature would take us back to Joseph Schumpeter, regarded by many as the creator of the term 'innovation,' who saw it as one of three key stages in the development of progress and of technological progress in particular.

The three stages, as he saw it, are invention, innovation and diffusion, with invention tied up with solving a technological or scientific problem, innovation depending on the solving of a commercial problem and diffusion, the adoption process through an industry, following innovation. In our analysis, we are including invention in the term 'creativity'.

Back in 1931, Joseph Schumpeter defined an innovation as a 'cycle starting' concept of national/international significance (for example, the opening of a new market or the introduction of a new production method). Over the years the significance of the word 'innovation' has shrunk such that it now describes far less significant activities (for example, the enlargement of a product range), but always in the context of the commercial exploitation of new ideas.

In the business world, innovation is about companies coming up with new products and new processes that enable them more effectively to compete and survive, and various authors have looked at how and why innovation occurs. A great deal has been written and we suggest that there are five very important signposts in the literature:

- Innovation occurs because it is nurtured and permitted by the organisation.
- Innovation occurs because certain companies see it as the best mechanism for them to survive and grow.
- Innovation can only properly take place given an appropriate opportunity and a supportive combination of factors.
- Innovation depends on a firm's ability to adopt, assimilate and exploit external knowledge.
- Innovation should be focused on the key aspects of a business.

Some of the case studies, particularly those for large firms, look impressive, but what do the findings mean for the smaller firm? The smaller firm might look towards the day when it can contemplate the core competence that Clive Prahalad and Gary Hamel saw as 'the key to world-class leadership,' but for now it may only have core skills or even key individuals. The most important factors for the smaller companies are the key parts played by chief executive officers in setting the goals and creating the climate for innovation, and the most serious barriers are lack of cash and staff. Of course, lack of cash and staff may also be general problems, but they bear down most heavily on the smaller firm.

Innovation is about change and the change must be well managed if the company is to benefit from it. Organic systems are 'high energy' systems. It takes a strong leader to maintain an organic approach, particularly when some parts of the organisation appear to have stable conditions (where some mechanistic approach would appear to offer efficient management) and where newly acquired staff may have a non-organic culture.

Chief executive officers and senior managers are involved with change created by themselves and imposed from outside of their organisation. They must be able to deal with both expansive and contractive change and ensure (if they wish their company to grow) that their attitudes and strategies do not produce contractive change. The task is difficult enough and those managers who regard themselves as being sufficiently skilled to manage change reactively rather than from the starting point of a business plan build in an extra degree of difficulty for themselves.

A good business planning session will provide managers with answers to the following questions:

1. Is the company operating with a low or high global awareness?
2. Is management creating an environment of expansive or contractive change?
3. How is management responding to externally imposed change, both favourable and unfavourable?
4. Is the company's strategy coherent and appropriate given its ambitions, strengths and marketplace?

Change is inevitable; progress is not and the magnitude and direction of change which is selected (and which thus determines the entropy vector) is critical.

Woolly and creative thinkers

But let us return to the issue of creativity. Innovation as a process is well documented and various management techniques can be taught to improve a company's performance in that process. Yet, forming new ideas and introducing them is necessary for the survival of any business. A business that does not develop new products will be overtaken by its competitors. So all businesses need creative thinkers—but how do you recognise them amongst the masses and the woolly thinkers?

Creativity is about seeing opportunities that others miss. For the cartoonist it can be a surreal play on words; for those in business, maybe a new opportunity to gain market share.

A woolly thinker is easy to spot; he or she lacks focus and definition and drifts in the murk. We could characterise them by suggesting that they would say: 'One plus one equals a banana, what time did you say it was?' In other words, the analysis is confused and they just get it plain wrong, like a photo-copier that shreds instead of copying a document. There is output but it is not the required output. In Boltzmann terms this is an undesirable macro state.

On the other hand, a creative thinker can be expected to go beyond the expected. We might imagine he or she saying something along the lines of 'One plus one equals two but it can also equal eleven and if you turn one of the 1s through 90 degrees it will equal T.' If you think about it you can represent zero by two 1s lying on their side at the top and the bottom and two 1s end to end for each side. Sort of like:

Then, if you make each of those 1s an LCD or something similar, you can have a display that goes 0123456789, depending on which of the 1s you energise. Sometimes the creative thinker is off the wall and, if you meet one of these at a cocktail party, you need to have your wits about you, say 'Well done' and make an exit. Sometimes, however, the idea is not as barmy as it might at first seem and you may just have got the gem you need for business success. ...

Creative thinkers are of great value to business, though no single business can cope with many of them. Many small businesses fail to grow because they are the brainchild of a creative thinker whose interest in the logical development of a single idea always comes second to the excitement of starting a new one.

Both woolly thinkers and creative thinkers are unconstrained and therefore, in principle, high entropy people. The first is unconstrained by discipline, the second by conformity and convention. Help people to break out of conventional linear logic, help them to make lateral steps and there is the promise of progress.

However, it is counterproductive to encourage woolly thinking by allowing people to dispense with common sense, concentration and a basic logical framework. Then disorder will be the consequence. Again, we see an example of where entropy on its own gives but a partial story; the key is the entropy vector. Increasing entropy through release from conformity and convention produces a positive outcome, but increase entropy still further by removing all focus and logical structure and disordered, useless ideas will be the result.

Incidentally, the process of creative thinking may look random but it is governed by clear basic rules. This makes it a chaotic process in the modern scientific meaning of the word, which is that the outcome of a process is unpredictable although well-defined and well-known laws govern it. A simple example of chaos is the balancing of a pencil on its point. It will always fall over but we cannot predict which way it will fall despite knowing that its fall is governed by the laws of gravity and of equilibrium of forces.

It is clear that encouraging one's workforce to be woolly in their thinking is a poor strategy, whereas encouraging creativity is positive. One way of testing the starting point—of seeing what level of morale, interest, creativity or woolliness exists—is to introduce a suggestion box system into the company. A low weekly response indicates disinterest and low morale, maybe as well as a possible lack of creative thinking. A high response is encouraging—but how many of the replies are woolly rather than genuinely creative? The trick now is to establish a worthwhile reward structure and give incentive for creativity. Creative ideas are the seeds of innovation. Do not be cheap—pay as much as you can afford and not as little as you can get away with. But which ideas are creative and which are woolly?

Sometimes the answer to that question is obvious, but sometimes it is not. Can we find a clue as to how to answer it by considering other environments where creativity is imperative? Nature, for example?

Nature is very creative. The mechanism is essentially interpolative through rearrangement of basic building blocks or pieces of information in the form of molecular structures or genes. The result is a high degree of diversity in the solutions and nature uses evolution to select solutions that best fit the need. Here again the entropy vector is at work. The continuous renewal of bio-diversity is increasing disorder and entropy. Nature controls the entropy vector by restricting diversity through survival of the fittest as part of the evolutionary process. Consequently, or at least by analogy if we can trust it, to innovate successfully it is important to create a diversity of ideas; but a good business or organisation must also use a suitable selection procedure. Creative ideas must 'fit the need' and the only way to separate them from the woolly ones is by careful questioning and testing.

Innovation, as a process, can be complex and iterative and there is rarely a straightforward linear development. Nevertheless, most researchers agree that there is some sequence to the basic process and there is a range of management methods for monitoring progress. The stage/gate approach of Robert Cooper is a good starting point, though the extent to which his approach is systematised depends on the size of the company. In principle this involves breaking the process down into clearly defined stages and having a formal review meeting with a 'gatekeeper' before the project passes to the next stage. At the very simplest level there needs to be an evaluation of ideas at the start of the innovation process and a mapping of them and their potential to the company's strengths and ambitions. In this way, only the new concepts and ideas that best fit the business plan progress to products.

A touch on the tiller, or even a hard tack to starboard, is needed to ensure that the entropy vector is both positive (implying increasing entropy) and harnessed to a level that is manageable and profitable. Of course the heavy hand on the tiller—or the over-cautious foot on the brake—defines a vector that is not positive enough. A second generation company that we know is run by a very pleasant managing director who has introduced a sensible, rigorous and efficient innovation control process—his personal variant on the stage/gate system. The trouble is, he is so cautious at the first gate that creativity is all but stamped out.

Creating creativity

How can you encourage the creation of new and diverse ideas? Of course, there is a saying that there are no new ideas, only recycled ones. There is an element of truth in this and thus external awareness, links to higher education and listening to customers are important strategies. However, it is too cynical to see this as the whole story and successful companies tend also to be inventive companies.

It is also true that many revolutionary discoveries and inventions have been made accidentally—we may call to mind the discovery by Roentgen of curious shapes on his photographic plate when he accidentally left his hand in the way and the consequent invention of X-ray radiography. [Actually the real event was a little more complicated. Back in 1895, Wilhelm Conrad Roentgen, a German physicist, was studying cathode rays in a high-voltage, gaseous-discharge tube. Despite the fact that the tube was encased in a black cardboard box, a barium-platinocyanide screen, inadvertently lying nearby, emitted fluorescent light whenever the tube was in operation. After conducting further experiments, Roentgen determined that the fluorescence was caused by invisible radiation of a more penetrating nature than ultraviolet rays. He named the invisible radiation 'X-rays' because of its unknown nature.]

However, we do not need to sit around waiting for accidents to happen and, indeed, most 'accidental' discoveries, like Roentgen's X-rays, are made in the process of experimentation. Theoretical science can free us from depending on accidental discovery by showing us where to look and in testing out theories. Karl Popper would tell us that only if a theory is testable is it scientific and the fate of most if not all hypotheses and theories is to be tested and found false. He would also tell us: 'Our knowledge would not have grown as it has unless in our search for confirming instances we accidentally hit upon a counter-instance.'

You can promote creativity by ordering and re-ordering the data that you have in new ways that will highlight the areas where experimentation might prove fruitful. You have to experiment to make accidents happen. These do not need to be physical experiments. Physicists and mathematicians are fond of thought or mind experiments. Architects and designers tend to experiment on paper by drawing and sketching. The modern tool is the computer.

The computer is widely used in engineering for simulating machines before building a prototype. These forms of experimentation are open to all of us and we must make the appropriate choice for our circumstances.

Clearly, sketching or computer modelling will not help us to develop a new, ready-to-cook meal. This involves experimenting in the kitchen.

We mentioned earlier that creative thinkers tend to be poor at the logical development of a single idea. This is partly because new questions arise from every problem solved. So, as fast as creative thinkers have new ideas, fresh avenues of exploration open up to them. Most of us follow well-worn paths of thought but creative thinkers tend to go down paths that are infrequently trampled on. Too many creative thinkers in an organisation, boldly thinking where no one has thought before, leads to a lack of focus. On the other hand, these thought processes, which often go off at a tangent, can lead to interesting and unexpected conclusions, so the odd wild card in the organisation is a good thing.

How do you spot the overgrown path or even the new route through the virgin territory? If you stand on the ground at the edge of a wooded mountain and look for a route to the other side, you will not see it. However, if you hop into the nearest helicopter or hot air balloon and take a slow flight over the mountain, then you will be able to identify the best route to the other side. You have added a dimension to your view and the extra dimension helps to identify the solution.

There is another example in knot theory. A rope lying loose but unknotted on the ground in three-dimensional space can be straightened out by pulling the ends; but when the two-dimensional image or picture of the rope is considered, we do not know whether it can be straightened out because 'knots' and overlaps appear identical.

Two-dimensional knots have tied up design engineers in the past but in recent years the extra dimension has been provided with a three-dimensional image produced in a computer-aided drawing (CAD) package. The argument is even more obvious with rapid prototyping technology and the advent of rapid prototyping machines, which are akin to three-dimensional printers. They allow engineering drawings to be converted into wax or plastic models in a few minutes, so that designers can work with three dimensions instead of the two dimensions of the flat screen or paper.

Knot or not?

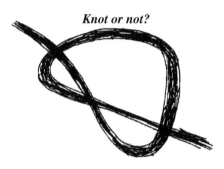

So, one way to increase creativity is to stretch your imagination or consciousness to an extra dimension—add an extra degree of freedom, become less constrained. Of course, the common parlance is 'lateral thinking', but this implies 'sideways' as opposed to 'straight-ahead', whereas we are suggesting adding an extra dimension so that you can 'see' all at once the sideways and straight-ahead paths as well as everything in between.

Clearly, some people have a natural disposition to do this and suitable technology will help—the rapid prototyping machines, for example—but we can all promote creativity by increasing the entropy involved in our thought processes. This means releasing some of the constraints and encouraging unconventional suggestions. Many people are capable of some degree of lateral or unconstrained thinking but are often inhibited from expressing those ideas precisely because the ideas are unconventional and they do not want to be seen as non-conformist.

Brainstorming sessions are known to be a good way of encouraging people to express these ideas, which often stimulate other people to produce further creative steps. The term 'brainstorming' seems particularly inappropriate, conjuring up a picture of well-drilled troops converging on an under-defended citadel. What we want is a much more relaxed environment where the walls melt away in the noonday sun and the inhabitants flood out of the darkened streets into the meadows and fields. Omar Khayyam had the right idea when he almost said 'a loaf of bread, a glass of wine and creativity'.

In our experience, a successful session requires a number of vital ingredients. These include: a means of releasing people's inhibitions (a good bottle of wine to accompany a light meal works well in our experience!); a good knowledge of the existing, enabling technology (it can be useful to have a few short presentations at the start to set the scene); one or two naturally creative people to stimulate the discussion or raise the entropy; and a good chairperson to distil the useful ideas and concepts or to keep control of the entropy vector.

Creativity is risky and expensive. The high entropy involved makes the outcome difficult to predict. Good creativity may generate an impressive diversity of ideas but only a few can be allowed to pass through the initial gate into the innovation process and even fewer will make it as successful product developments. This makes creativity and innovation an inefficient and expensive process and some organisations seek to minimise the level of innovation.

A 'me too' approach to development is cheaper and less risky. This removes the creative process by waiting to see what someone else does and then copying. Followership as opposed to leadership. Yet a business with a high level of creativity and innovation is far more likely to succeed and all lists of visionary or successful or 'winning' companies have creativity tucked in amongst their core characteristics.

The trick is a controllable entropy vector; a resultant course made up of almost unconstrained creativity and, in equal measure, an efficient and well-controlled innovation process. The success of 3M is often cited in this context and it is a good example.

Another one is Racal, a company identified as one of the UK's top companies in 1984 in Walter Goldsmith and David Clutterbuck's book *The Winning Streak* and in the news in January 2000 with reports of its successful sale to Thomson-CSF by Sir Ernest Harrison, Racal's chairman and long-time leader. Racal powered to a world leadership position in the defence equipment area in the late 1960s, by creative development of new products ('we simply went against the trend and gave people what they wanted') whilst keeping a tight rein on development and in particular development costs. 'If he doesn't know the targeted cost of the development, he is not the engineer I need.' It might not need saying, but to blend a creative approach and a well-controlled innovation process usually requires someone special at the top (in Racal's case, Sir Ernest Harrison).

Racal's success has continued and, to illustrate this, the newspaper article of January 2000 says that if you had invested £1000 in Racal shares in 1961 and had reinvested dividends and kept spinout shares, then your holding would be worth £15.6 million. Wow!

Technopy

Of course, mankind has been very inventive for many centuries. People have surmised that this inventive streak has been driven by curiosity, or adversity, or competition. Whilst each of these drivers has probably played a role that has varied with time, entropy has also played a major role. In an irreversible process, entropy always increases. Technology in its broadest sense is a direct equivalent to entropy. The total wealth of technology only increases and each strand of technology follows its characteristic trajectory. Once something has been invented it cannot be un-invented, though it can remain undeveloped for many years. For example, liquid crystals graced the patent literature for many decades before the first liquid crystal displays became commercially available. Even the mundane zip fastener took thirty years from the generation of the idea to the broad scale launch.

So the technology available to society is steadily increasing, like 'natural entropy'. Of course, it is possible to hide or suppress a discovery from a sector of society, but this involves the imposition of constraints and a lowering of entropy that is only possible in a closed system, such as the defence industry.

The analogy can be extended because increasing entropy involves removing constraints and, similarly, technology removes constraints. There are many examples of this; for instance, today, if you want to send a letter to someone in another town you can choose from many means of communication. These vary from electronic mail, taking a fraction of a second, to letter post, taking a day or more. Three hundred years ago, the speed of letter post was a significant constraint on business. The advent of mechanised transport networks significantly removed this constraint and the age of electronic communication has all but done away with it.

We will recall from earlier chapters that the preferred state for a thermodynamic system is an equilibrium state, which maximises entropy. In technology terms, our quest to invent or discover new technology will cease only when we know and have discovered everything. This would be a form of equilibrium, since there could be no further changes from this state and it would represent a maximum level of technology. However, it is questionable whether such a state will exist, since the limit of the physical universe and of science is probably beyond our comprehension.

As Popper reminded us, we do not even know whether our theories are correct, we can merely justify our preference for one over another. All the observable evidence that fitted Newton's theories also fits Einstein's, but Einstein does more and explains truths that are inconsistent with Newton's explanation. Yet no theory can be relied upon to give the final truth and no point on a technology trajectory can be assumed to be the ultimate. It is likely that we will always be moving gradually closer to this maximum level of technology in ever-decreasing steps, i.e. asymptotically.

New technology or improvements in technology effectively devalue the products and devices that you already possess—take a look at the value of the computer you bought last year. This is the same effect that entropy increases have on free energy, for if entropy is always increasing, free energy or exergy must always be decreasing. As mentioned earlier, you will realise this to your chagrin if you leave your Walkman batteries out in the back garden for twelve months and then hope they will work.

In the case of technology, this devaluing effect tends to lead us into believing that the latest discoveries are the most significant. The number of directions in which technology is advancing simultaneously also affects our perspective. If we return to the concept of advancing the frontiers of knowledge, then the larger our knowledge becomes the longer the boundary around it and so the greater is the potential for pushing out the boundary and extending our knowledge.

So the analogy between entropy and technology fits on a number of fronts and leads to the concept of technology entropy, or 'technopy'. An organisation with high technopy has lots of exciting new ideas and products that will expand the market and give the organisation an advantage compared with their competitors. The competition between companies and the demands from consumers lead to constant increase in the technopy of the marketplace. The marketplace has an average or natural level of technopy that increases with time. Individual businesses must achieve and maintain a technopy level that is higher than the natural level in order to prosper.

We can examine this concept of technopy with the help of a figure, but before we do, let us just recap on the behaviour of entropy in systems. In an isolated closed system (i.e. a system whose volume and internal energy are fixed) the entropy tends to a maximum value. In an open system where volume and energy may increase, the entropy will increase without showing any tendency to a maximum. By 'tending to a maximum' we mean that it will increase at a slower and slower rate as time passes and will only reach a maximum value after an infinite passage of time.

So, what can we say about a marketplace? Clearly, it is not a closed system, for new entrants may appear and each product improvement may possibly increase the volume (measured in terms of total sales volume).

A naturally upward trend in entropy in a closed system becomes a steeper and/or longer curve in an open one. With time, the opportunity decreases for new entrants (or even existing competitors) to produce a step change with a striking new product. Eventually, the curve will flatten and technopy will tend to a maximum as the potential to invent and develop new things decreases.

We may consider some companies at any moment in time to rise above what we may call the 'natural technopy' curve of the marketplace and others to fall below. This natural technopy curve lies in a band of what we might call 'user-acceptable products'. Companies that travel an entropy vector, or a technopy vector that takes them below this band, will find themselves making products that the market doesn't want or, in the extreme case, these companies may even fail to make product at all. As time passes, new products and new companies replace old ones. Look at the technology for writing. Not too many quill manufacturers exist today and the development from the first manual Remington typewriter (you got to the fourth line of typing before the paper emerged and you could begin to see what was typed) to today's laptops (which correct our spelling even as we write) has involved many products and many companies. James Utterback tells this and several other technology development stories in his book *The Dynamics of Innovation*.

We can draw a simple diagram to help picture this. Time is on the horizontal axis, and technical entropy (technopy) on the vertical one. There is a natural technopy curve for the chosen marketplace and, around it, a band of user-acceptable products.

In the diagram below, we have sketched out technopy curves for five types of company (A to E), each with a different curve shape, or trajectory. They can be characterised as follows:

(A) An innovative company that gets it right and then continues to innovate, keeping ahead of the field for well into the life of the technology. Maybe another burst of innovative creativity will give it another market leadership position; or maybe as the technology matures it must settle for continuous improvement that keeps it at or ideally just above the natural technopy curve.

(B) A highly innovative company. This time with a development that enables user-acceptable products to be made well ahead of technically equivalent competition. But the absence of continuing development and innovation means that others can catch up, especially if there is no protection of intellectual property, through patenting for example. Ultimately the highly advanced products become obsolete and the company fails.

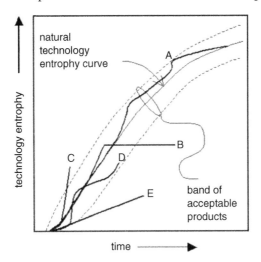

(C) A highly innovative company that achieves a technology development well ahead of its time. But too far ahead. The market is not ready for it and the premature launch of unwanted products leads to disaster.

(D) A company that makes an effort to innovate and stays approximately on the natural curve. It will make user-acceptable products and can be assured of some sales but it will not be a market leader.

(E) A company with a poor rate of innovation. The natural entropy is not going into technological development—maybe the management information system is chaotic, for you cannot escape increasing entropy. Whatever the reason, it is not making user-acceptable products. It will fail.

The crux of our model is that the natural technopy curve is the inevitable rate of change in a market and companies that fall off the pace end up with obsolete products and as a consequence low profits and a bleak future. Let us move away from idealised examples of companies and look at a real example. We suggested earlier in the book that when the thinking gets tough we should take a break and brew up a cup of tea, so let us go back and have a closer look at the electric kettle. There has been a continuous process of innovation during the last twenty years or so, which has brought about a kettle that is cool to the touch, docks onto a base containing the power connection and switches itself off when the water is boiling. Any company that has not kept up with these advances in technology would be faced with falling sales and eventually an obsolete product.

What of those companies which create new products and processes? They are working at a higher rate of change or a technopy acquisition at a steeper gradient than the natural curve. If their creativity is successful they have got to a point on the technopy curve some time before such a point may be 'naturally' reached. A period of time will elapse before their competitors can catch with them up by other technological developments, but, if they do not protect their invention, there is no reason why a competitor cannot copy the change and very quickly be at the same technology level.

Good protection, by a patent, will effectively block such a 'me too' activity, forcing the competitor to wait or alternatively embark upon a higher technopy curve to 'get round' the protected property. The higher the technopy curve, the greater the risk, and some companies may decide it is best to accept a lesser market share; others may attempt the high risk path and find themselves stranded without a user-acceptable product on offer. After all, not all technological developments are successful and there are risks of going outside the 'band of user-acceptable products' on the high technopy side, just as on the low technopy side.

The earlier example of the electric kettle will serve our purpose again, for it is a particularly good example. Whilst there have been a series of innovations to give us the jug kettle of today (i.e. modest surges of technopy as competitive companies sought to keep above the line of natural technopy), the original idea represented a radical innovation (a high gradient lurch away from the middle). The original idea represented a real opportunity for a company to get ahead of the natural technopy curve and Redring, a subsidiary of GEC, tried to do this.

Sadly, the company, which at that time was an engineering company mainly producing heat exchangers, found that the kettle presented problems both in manufacturing and marketing. It needed skills and competencies in plastics processing to make the kettle and skills and experience in marketing to sell it. By the time Redring had gained these skills and competencies, it no longer had the market to itself and was able only to secure a small share.

We should make one final point. In the scenarios sketched out above and in the figure, we have not allowed for any discontinuity caused by a new technology that advances the market into a new plane or sphere before the original technology is fully mature. Such discontinuities do of course occur—the jet engine and the personal computer are obvious examples—and can complicate the neatest of management models.

On the technopy curve, the discontinuity will be an example of scenario C writ large and fortunate enough or attractive enough to gain sufficient user acceptance so as to avoid failure. The new curve set by this transforming innovation will be steep and for a while seemingly indisposed to tend to a maximum. However, without further discontinuity, the pace will slacken off and a maximum will be approached. One is tempted to say 'as night follows day'—but that is rather too ordered an analogy for a discussion on entropy!

Coffee and a matrix

Entropy can only increase, resulting in a release of constraints, which brings about change. Technology behaves in a directly analogous manner, so we introduced the concept of technopy. Our level of technology is continuously increasing and releasing us from constraints. They say that change is inevitable except from vending machines and, in fact, the coffee vending machine is an interesting if difficult example. As an invention or design it represents an increase in technology entropy or technopy. For its customers it clearly offers choice and hence removes constraint, implying higher entropy; this is a common feature of new technology.

'Change is inevitable except from vending machines.'

But by providing a service that can be equated with a potential to do work, the vending machine is also associated with low entropy. It is clearly a highly ordered set of parts, suggesting a low entropy system. Finally, it heats water and mixes it with coffee, increasing the entropy of the water and coffee. So, which of these is correct? The answer is 'all of them', but at each stage we have defined our system differently. For the design, the system is the technology portfolio of society; for the customer, the system is the marketplace. In terms of the potential to do work and the molecular arrangement in the machine, the system is the vending machine itself. In common with all modern devices, it is well ordered, and this has involved lowering entropy locally by expending energy, but raising entropy and disorder outside the local system, usually in the form of pollution. When the coffee is being made the system is defined as the water and coffee, and the exergy is supplied via the electrical socket.

Engineering students, when they are being taught thermodynamics, are told repeatedly about the importance of defining their system appropriately. It is also important in the business context and many a business strategy meeting will begin with the question 'What business are we in?' Defining boundaries is an important task of the patent attorney and the concept of the intellectual property portfolio allows us to define a system consisting of known technology and to have company and public domains. We will not have changed anything physically, but this ordering of our thinking, this reduction of mental entropy, is important in enabling us to make better decisions when we do begin to make real changes. More of mental entropy in Chapter 10.

To conclude, it is important to remember that the entropy vector implies that all organisations must innovate to survive. This means successfully introducing new ideas and products. However, innovation alone will not ensure success, only survival. To be a leader, organisations must also show creativity by forming new ideas. Through a combination of creativity and innovation, an organisation can pull away from the pack for a short time. Continuous creativity and innovation are needed to maintain a lead. The process of creativity is risky and is associated with increasing entropy by releasing thought processes from convention and conformity. This should lead to a diversity of ideas and the entropy vector must be harnessed through selecting only the best ideas for the innovation process.

Perhaps we should end this chapter by summarising these thoughts in a two-by-two matrix, where we characterise organisations in four broad groups, depending on their degree of creativity and innovation.

Low creativity and low innovation goes nowhere; high creativity on its own has all the appearance of an inventions factory. Good innovation and low creativity has the prospect of a survivable 'me too' operation but market leadership demands both high creativity and high innovation—a vector made up of almost unconstrained creativity and severely constrained innovation.

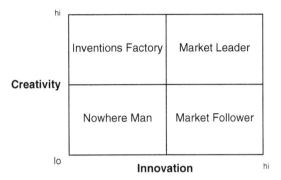

Notes and quotes

- Omar Khayyam lived in the eleventh/twelfth century and was a Persian mathematician and astronomer and the author of one of the world's best-known works of poetry. The standard misquote of Omar Khayyam is 'a flask of wine, a loaf of bread and thou'. The actual quatrain from his famous *Rubaiyat* goes something along the following lines:

A gourd of red wine and a sheaf of poems—
A bare subsistence, half a loaf no more—
Supplied us two alone in the free desert;
What Sultan could we envy on his throne.

Poetry, eh? Don't ya just love it?

- Innovation

There is a great deal of literature on this. The following sources informed the preparation of this chapter.

T. Burns and G.M. Stalker, *The Management of Innovation* (Tavistock, London, 1961).

Back in the late 1950s or early 1960s, Tom Burns and George Stalker (1961) looked at the performance of a number of British electronics companies and suggested that different management systems (which they dubbed 'organic' rather than 'mechanistic') were needed by organisations when they faced new challenges and rapidly changing markets and technologies.

M.E. Porter, *Competitive Strategy* (The Free Press, London, 1980).
Of course, other factors are also important and, in 1980, Michael
Porter focused attention on competitive strategy and the need to see
innovations in that context.

W.M. Cohen and D.A. Levinthal (1994), 'Fortune favors the
prepared firm', *Management Science*, Vol. 40, No. 2, Feb. (1994).
A key area is a firm's ability to acquire outside knowledge, and the
capacity to exploit such knowledge depends on a firm's 'absorptive
ability'—a set of closely related abilities to evaluate the technological
and commercial potential of knowledge in a particular domain, assimilate it and apply it to commercial ends.

W.C. Kim and R. Mauborge, 'The strategic logic of high growth',
Harvard Business Review, 75, No.1 (1997).
Whilst innovation may occur and must occur generally, the only
companies that truly succeed are those that embark on what they call
strategic innovation and actually break out of the constraints of their
environment and industry.

S.-O. Hansén and J. Wakonen, 'Innovation: a winning solution', *Int.
J. Technology Management*, Vol. 13, No. 4 (1997) pp. 345–58. See this
for a fuller review of Schumpeter.

C. Prahalad and G. Hamel, 'Core competencies of the corporation',
Harvard Business Review, May–June 1990, p. 79.

J. Tidd, J. Bessant and K. Pavitt, *Managing Innovation* (Wiley, 1997).
A very readable text, including the Redring kettle story (see D. Walker,
1986, 'The Redring Kettle Case', Open University Design and
Innovation Course, for the primary source).

- Creativity? Well, there is plenty of literature on this too.
Try *Adaptors and Innovators: Styles of Creativity and Problem
Solving*, revised edition; edited by Michael Kirton (Routledge,
London, and New York, 1994).

There is also, not surprisingly, a great deal of psychological study
and dissection of aspects of creativity such as incubation and insight.
For those wanting a helpful skim across the surface, try *Developing
Creativity in Organisations*, by Michael A. West (BPS Books,
1997). We should also refer you to *Creativity and Problem Solving
at Work*, by Tudor Rickards (Gower, 1997). Our style of brainstorming
is very personalised. He describes more rigorous procedures that
might be more widely applicable. He also (among other things) rec-
ommends that you develop the habit of saying 'yes and' in preference
to 'yes but', and helps you identify your 'stuckness' and gives helpful
techniques to be creative, become unstuck and move on.

- *The Winning Streak*, by Walter Goldsmith and David Clutterbuck (Penguin Business, London, 1984). An attempt, and a good one, to do with UK top companies what Tom Peters did in the US with *In Search of Excellence*.
- Robert G. Cooper, *Winning at New Products: Accelerating the Process from Idea to Launch*, 2nd ed. (Addison-Wesley, Reading, Mass., 1993).
- Karl R. Popper? More of him in Chapter 10. An excellent introduction to Popper's work is provided by Bryan Magee in *Popper* (Fontana Modern Masters, Fontana/Collins, London, 1973).
- *Mastering the Dynamics of Innovation*, by James M. Utterback (Harvard Business School Press, Cambridge, Mass., 1996). Source of our typewriter comments and well worth a read.

9

Risk and Entropy

ontRe-pRenur • winning the risk game • boundaries and vision • sins of omission/commission • elephants, rabbits, barbecues and the cost of grass

There are some very good books on risk management and it is not the intention here to summarise them or to offer a potted get-rich-quick checklist. Neither do we intend to get into discussions on risk that relate to health and safety issues. Rather, what we seek to do is to look at some business practice issues involving risk and consider what role entropy plays.

We have selected four aspects of business life. First we will look at the issue of start-up and entrepreneurs; then we will move on to under-achievement; then to time and people management and the issue of efficiency; and finally to business failure.

ontRe-pRenur

Let us begin with business start-up and entrepreneurship—not that all businesses which start up are entrepreneurial or that entrepreneurship is the exclusive domain of the small business. Just what is an entrepreneur? We might guess by the sound of it that it is a French word and Peter Drucker, in his book *Innovation and Entrepreneurship*, tells us that a French economist, Jean Baptiste Say, coined it back around 1800. Drucker quotes Say: 'The entrepreneur shifts economic resources out of an area of lower into an area of higher productivity and greater yield.'

This expression resonates with school-days physics—the heat pump (including the common refrigerator) shifts heat out of an area of lower into an area of higher temperature, and we all know from the second law of thermodynamics that you do not get this kind of thing happening without the application of external work. We will have more of Drucker in a moment, but we should note that later in the same book he suggests first that the entrepreneur achieves his 'shift' by innovation and second that 'innovation is work'.

Say's definition does not tell us who this entrepreneur is and since Say coined the term two hundred years ago, there has been endless confusion over the definitions of 'entrepreneur' and 'entrepreneurship'.

When I use a word it means just what I choose it to mean – neither more nor less

Humpty Dumpty explains. ... (From: Lewis Carroll, *Alice Through the Looking Glass.*)

But then, confusion over the meaning of words taken from the French is to be expected, for the English and French have a love–hate relationship with each other's language. On the one hand, the French will make back-handed compliments along the lines that they are pleased that English and not French is becoming the 'international language' since they would hate French to be so ill-treated. On the other, they will pick up English words and phrases because there is no simple French equivalent. The French commentators at a soccer match talk of a 'corner'. The alternative is the French expression, which takes longer to get through than the kick itself. The English, of course, regard their own language as the obvious choice, rich in simple and straightforward words, yet at almost any opportunity they will borrow a word from France if it helps the speaker to sound more educated, more worldly, more important. 'Entrepreneur' is a case in point and indeed is an example of how the English so much like the sound of a word that they change its meaning to enable it to be used more often. Bob's desk dictionary was published in 1965—it has been with him for longer than he has had an office to put a desk in—and the word 'entrepreneur' is listed:

[*ontRe-pRenur*] *n* (*Fr*) a contractor; a promoter, *esp* of theatrical or musical performances.

Frankly, that definition does not help at all, except maybe in the sense that 'contractor' implies someone who does something and 'promoter' someone who develops a market. Indeed, by the 1983 edition, the shorter *OED* included 'a contractor acting as an intermediary between capital and labour'. Coincidentally, 'entrepreneur' is listed on the same page as 'entropy'.

A common, current use of the word 'entrepreneur' is in the sense of someone who starts a new business—usually by identifying a market opportunity and attacking it with a great deal of energy and at the risk of losing his or her money and often house as well. Drucker would have us consider this further and separate out those who simply hope to cash in on an established trend from those who create a new customer and a new market. For example, the couple that open another restaurant or deli in a US suburb as opposed to McDonald's, who asked what the value to the customer was, standardised the product, based training on the analysis of the work done and set the standards. Entrepreneurs change the marketplace.

Drucker asserts that innovation is the specific tool of entrepreneurs and, in common with Say, that the entrepreneur upsets and disorganises. Joseph Schumpeter, the German economist credited with introducing the first definition of innovation, also refers back to Say and talks of entrepreneurial activity as creative destruction and postulates that 'dynamic disequilibrium brought on by the innovative entrepreneur is the norm of a healthy economy'. To paraphrase the advice given to Steve Martin's character in the film *Parenthood*, 'You better hold on tight, boy, life is a roller-coaster.'

The links to entropy are very apparent and were Clausius here, he might suggest: 'The entropy of the universe is increasing and entrepreneurs are increasing the rate.' In the previous chapter, we introduced the idea of technopy to help discuss this process of innovation.

Whether or not we accept Drucker's distinction between market follower and market maker as one of kind or one of degree, it is clear that the entrepreneur is street-wise, market-focused and takes risks. The person is distinguishable from the professional starting up his or her own practice, because the entrepreneur sees and seizes a market opportunity rather than incorporates or forms a practice as a natural step in a process that involves education, training and professional development. The normal entrepreneurial business is also usually distinguishable from the high-tech start-up too, as the motivation is to make money quickly—and at risk—from a market opportunity rather than to be involved in a technical development. The distinction is blurred as some entrepreneurs have been successful in picking up a technical development that was nearing fruition and taking it forward.

Winning at the risk game

The word 'risk' keeps creeping in and entrepreneurs have been defined as 'risk-takers'. This oversimplifies the case but it is a characteristic—the willingness to take a risk and the ability to succeed. By definition, they are successful risk-takers, otherwise they go bust and are no longer entrepreneurs. This implies successful risk avoidance, since the second law militates against risks working out. Put another way, they have to focus on the risks they need to take and eschew those they do not. The ability to focus on the key issues is another key aspect of an entrepreneur. It assists in enabling them to become successful, yet if they do not have the ability to widen their focus it limits their further growth.

For all business ventures there are strategies for getting from A to B, each with its own associated risks, rewards and costs. The skill of the entrepreneur is to balance these. The entrepreneur needs to be sufficiently confident of the rewards to take financial risks that many of the rest of us would not contemplate; to be sufficiently market-focused to change direction and switch product ideas whilst many of the rest of us would be too emotionally tied to our original idea; to be sufficiently able/bold/street-wise/commercial to organise purchases, people and resources in a way that minimises cost, where the rest of us would spend more money.

We have identified entrepreneurship to be based on an economic theory that is congruent with entropy. Is there any hint in all of this of a particular entropy vector? We think there is, because some risks are avoidable. On the other hand, some of the risks are unavoidable—they must be incurred or the venture will not proceed, for we have defined entrepreneurialism as a risk-based activity. The successful entrepreneur will take steps to ensure that the other risks, the avoidable risks, are minimised if not eliminated. The risks he or she takes generate unknowns and effort must be placed in preventing other unknowns occurring. The entrepreneur constrains the system, applies order, and keeps it simple by the expedient of careful focus and ruthless selection. By minimising disorder—by taking the lowest possible entropy vector—the entrepreneur gives him or herself the best possible opportunity of identifying deviations from what was expected to happen and thus the best opportunity of making corrective change.

There is an additional entropy issue. We noted in an earlier chapter that the entropy change in cooling a slab of hot metal was highest when the cooling was done in one process and lowest when multiple cooling was employed. The zero entropy cooling process required an infinite number of steps, which would provide a system that was reversible. Not even the most effective entrepreneur can reverse their process but they do take the smallest possible steps—even though some of these steps would be too large for the less adventurous of us to contemplate. Within the context of their chosen mission, the steps are as small as possible. If you are setting up a new transatlantic airline, then you have no choice but to buy or lease one aircraft!

Parable of the talents

The second category of business risk is underachievement. Why do some organisations underachieve when in principle they look as likely to succeed and grow as the next? There will, of course, be a range of explanations. Consider the parable of the talents, a story told by Jesus. There are a variety of interpretations of this, but take the following simple approach for the moment. Three businesses each had a certain amount of resources. The businesses were different; the amounts of resources were different. Two of the businesses traded profitably and showed considerable capital growth whilst the other, the one with the least resources, took a more risk-averse course and stagnated. What conclusions can we draw? The business with the most resources makes the most money; the business that stagnated has the least resources; the business with the least to lose is the most risk-averse. Well, maybe, but there is a further conclusion and one that is relevant to our discussion here: some managers are more fearful of failure than of lack of success. To reset this in religious terminology, the sins of omission can outweigh the sins of commission.

The question goes deeper than just a manager's personal balance between taking action and not. There is considerable literature, particularly in the area of technology management and innovation, to suggest that it is the culture, systems, structure and controls of an organisation that prevent, deter, allow, encourage or propel an individual. 3M, a company with a rich history of innovative growth, identifies 'fear of failure' as a key barrier to innovation and reduces this by providing free work time during which staff can experiment without fear of their results being judged.

Taking on new products is risky but organisations underachieve if they do not. One can see cautious companies wishing to provide stable employment and to have resources carefully determined and made ready to exploit any new product taken on, yet underachieving because they fail to commit. A senior manager of a local company told us recently that he was unable to take advantage of a government-promoted scheme for 'world class manufacturing' despite the considerable subsidy and importance of the topic because none of the particular projects defined in the scheme matched the detail of the programme in his budget. His company policy was not to carry out work for which there was no budget provision. One might suggest that this particular style of corporate governance has a negative impact on innovation. For our purposes we would simply state that an over-constrained system—one that seeks too fervently to minimise entropy growth—is undesirable. Some resetting of the entropy vector towards a situation where companies can be more cavalier, grasp opportunities and see how they succeed is advantageous. As Richard Branson said in the 1998 UK Innovation Lecture: 'Sometimes you just have to go for it.' Virgin, his company, has made risk-taking a management style. Such a style is not for the faint-hearted and Richard Branson admits that during the first 18 years survival was the dominant task and that Virgin came close to 'going to the wall' several times. As he so delightfully puts it, it is only for the last decade or so that they have got 'over the wall'.

The initial record company grew dramatically by signing the Sex Pistols whilst traditional labels thought them too risky/outrageous. Three years later Virgin bought a second-hand aeroplane and Virgin Atlantic was born—not the safest or most obvious of company expansion decisions! So why is Virgin successful? Its senior managers talk of a decentralised, flat structure where a single decision-maker makes bold decisions. They talk of new business where the Virgin values of customer care, quality and value for money can make inroads. In their language, they look for the 'big bad wolf' markets. More recently, they have taken to turning round inefficient, run-down and demoralised organisations like the railways.

Virgin keep innovating to move the vision onwards; they repackage existing ideas; they recruit and retain a lot of enterprising minds. Managers say that Virgin is the closest you can get to being self-employed. They identify the lack of a blame culture and an environment where all are encouraged. 'All flourish under praise—all shrivel under criticism. You don't need to be told you've made a mistake,' says Richard Branson.

Virgin simply take more adventurous decisions. They set a course that takes them into high entropy waters. The overriding philosophy is that it is better to decide and act rather than prevaricate. The top management let staff make as many decisions as possible. They get ahead and stay ahead by massive leaps. They aim to be the best but to do this they have got to be willing to take risks; they need to delegate in order to grow.

Richard Branson admits to loving a challenge but Virgin's course is not set aimlessly for the unknown. There are some important constraints, some key criteria that put them on the right high entropy path. New ventures must promise substantial benefits—or, as Branson says, have a 'terrific upside'. They must also have a manageable downside. And how do you manage the downside? Well, for Virgin Atlantic, the deal on the aeroplane that they bought to start the venture was that Boeing would take it back after a year at a pre-agreed price if Virgin decided to pull out.

One final point about Virgin. The 17,000 or so people who work there do not work for an empire. The business is structured as a lot of separate companies. The key is to take time to find good people and then give them the freedom to achieve, be bold, stand out from the crowd, be visible and get noticed.

Elephants and rabbits

In part, this freedom to achieve, to change direction, to 'just go for it' is an issue of size. An elephant moves more slowly than a rabbit, eats more grass and is much more difficult to cook on a barbecue [sometimes you just don't have to take analogies too seriously]. In part, and the reason for the comments in this chapter, it is an issue of risk-taking and the benefits of entropy creation versus nicely and tightly constrained organisations where the high degree of order results in pitiful underachievement. Nationalised companies are often examples of underachievement, particularly, when compared with the often massive investment from the owner—you, the taxpayer.

The third category is time and people management and the issue of efficiency. To waste time is to waste money, because firstly staff are paid

Almost done!

for their time and secondly market opportunities are missed. It is easy for the small company to keep this in focus, but in larger companies where many people are doing indirect tasks the link is not always so clear. It can be difficult to interpret an activity in terms of an achievement, particularly a profit achievement.

Where there is no sense of achievement and no obvious link to profit generation, there is scope for waste. Take for example the task of managing a team. Do it badly and the efficiency of the team is poor. Manage people badly and you waste time, and wasted time is wasted money. Let us illustrate this with an example from our own laboratory and with a simple two-by-two matrix.

The task is to reorganise the laboratory. The objective is to move out of cramped, old space and into larger, better-equipped facilities in the same building. On the *y*-axis is the extent of planning from 'nothing is decided' to a complete frozen design. On the *x*-axis is involvement of staff from low to high.

Clearly, one option is for management to work out the plans and designs in some detail and then to hold a meeting to involve the staff. The route through the grid from the bottom-left-hand box is vertical and then horizontal.

Another option is to go horizontally first and hold a full team meeting at the planning stage and then to move vertically, by agreeing the plan with full team involvement. This second route is more difficult managerially in terms of steering the team towards a consensus and to ensure that

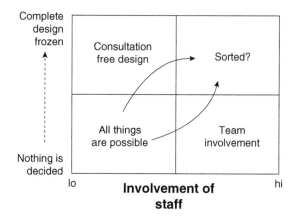

certain management requirements for the new laboratory are met. It does, however, offer an easier path to getting the new laboratory operating, for the team will feel involved and committed.

We have discussed this in terms of a two-by-two matrix but in fact there is a third dimension of quality. In two dimensions, the two routes go to the same top-right-hand-side box but the right-then-up route arrives at a different and higher quality level than the up-then-right route.

Both paths have risks attached. For one, the risk of not having the staff with you and thus the potential for delay, difficulty and waste. For the other, the risk for management of not looking purposeful and of not getting the laboratory designed as they deem best. Which route to choose? Managers talk of taking a calculated risk, but never explain how they calculate it so that we can check the calculation. Is it simply a guess? What, for that matter, has it to do with entropy? Well, actually, quite a lot.

Drawing boundaries and vision

First, a brief recap. The statistical mechanics definition of entropy refers to an abstract mathematical meaning of entropy that is related to probability and hence, according to the mathematics, entropy can both increase and decrease—things that are more likely to happen will happen but improbable things do occur, although you have to wait a very, very long time. This is Poincare's recurrence, which we have mentioned before. According to the statistical mechanics definition, the entropy of an event is the degree of uncertainty with which it can be predicted or specified. If we can constrain the appropriate variables, then the entropy or uncertainty can be reduced.

However, we also know from our thermodynamics understanding of free energy and entropy that the task of creating the constraints will involve increases in entropy as free energy will be used in this creation process. Quite simply, it is the way you define your system that will determine whether the entropy in it increases or decreases since, inescapably, the total entropy in the universe continues to increase. Mathematicians just love to define systems (ascribe boundary conditions in their language) and as a consequence introduce the spurious phenomenon of locally decreasing entropy.

Having said that, it can be useful to define systems quite tightly and by so doing it is possible to gain an understanding of what is happening in the system. So, to return to the task of redesigning the laboratory, we can consider a closed system and look at the different degrees of constraint that arise from the different routes involved.

The 'go right, then up' route begins with unconstrained change— we invite colleagues to become involved and to say what they wish. Unconstrained change is a high entropy route with associated high risk (what if staff will not accept management's ideas or staff proposals do not fit the design brief?), and with potentially high rewards (in this case a higher quality design and a greater commitment by staff to make the transition quickly and smoothly). More broadly, we can transfer the concept to other management tasks and suggest that unconstrained change (or unconstrained projects) is high-entropy, high-risk and has potentially high rewards.

Conversely, the up-then-right route is highly constrained change— essentially we decide on the design change and tell colleagues what they have to do. Highly constrained projects are low entropy, low risk and will only produce small improvements. For our laboratory, it will only include the managers' ideas of what is best, with the risk that even these improvements will only be partially implemented, as we will have to rely on others to implement our ideas. There is a high chance of getting the new laboratory set up relatively quickly but at a lower quality solution than might have been the case. A low entropy route can be a nicely ordered move to mediocrity.

In general, we might suggest that highly constrained projects are low entropy, low risk and will only produce small incremental impacts on profits. In contrast, management that allows its people a high degree of freedom and autonomy is likely to be on a higher entropy vector and to have maximum benefits. Clearly it also risks achieving a high degree of disorder and hence inefficiency so the argument can also be made the other way round. Staff need to be empowered in order to provide maximum benefits for the company but they need first to share the company vision and to be enjoined in mutual trust to avoid a spiral into disorder. The issue for management is not so much to decide when and where constraint is needed but rather to set and share the vision.

Coping with failure

The final category is the risk of failure. In this context something must be said about business plans, which are a way of avoiding too many unknowns. Business plans provide a way of trying to think ahead in order to organise (i.e. minimise) disorder in the way that a business is developed. They also provide a framework of proposed actions against which actual performance may be compared so that deviations can be identified and dealt with as early as possible. The entropy law tells us that entropy gain is minimised by carrying out a process in as large a number of steps as is practical. The objective is big, useful change and the best route is by controlled steps. Good business planning and the incrementalist approaches advocated by Mintzberg, Quinn and others are all soundly grounded in good science.

Back in the early 1980s management training consultants were already apologising for using the overworked expression 'people do not plan to fail but they fail to plan'. It is probably still overworked, so we should apologise too and it is certainly worth avoiding the repetition of that old piece of alliteration, 'professional planning prevents poor performance'. We raise the point about planning to fail because there is a reasonable argument that whilst no one should plan to fail, companies should plan for failure or, at the very least, plan for a waste. The entropy law tells us that in the real world when free energy is used to do work there is an increase in entropy and increasing entropy, as we know, represents an increase in disorder and a loss of efficiency.

Traditionally, engineers have always understood the significance of this and built safety factors into their calculations. Allowances, not just to be sure, but in recognition that in real situations there are always losses and unexpected factors. Murphy's law ('if something can go wrong, it will') is another glimpse of the underlying and inevitable truth of the second law. Thus, a correct plan will build in contingencies and with them sub-plans to deal with deviations that are even greater than the contingency provision.

Consider the task of establishing a major tourist attraction in a regional city by relocating treasures and historical artefacts that have been stored in museum vaults in the capital. The new attraction is built with much publicity and central government money and plans for its viability made on the basis of numbers of visitors per day at admission prices. There is huge optimism about profitability and hope for regional regeneration. There is a high level launch but then subsequent additional publicity—the news that there is an emergency meeting of trustees to decide what to do in the face of a worrying shortfall in visitors. The probable consequence, at least in the short term, will be an even more rapid fall-off in visitors—firstly as people stay away because they think it is closing down, because they do not wish to visit something that isn't very good and if other people aren't visiting it can't be very good (can it?), and secondly, because they think the trustees might respond by dropping the price, so it is worth waiting a few weeks. Yet there might be a fantastic building, a magnificent showcase for the artefacts. The problem is that the treasures and artefacts are not sufficiently interesting to attract the local (regional) population to make repetitive visits and the tourism business is not as robust as in the capital.

Hamlet plans his entropy vector.

No amount of planning will guarantee that people visit the tourist attraction but some care in planning for waste (in this case waste of overheads) might enable a cheaper system to be set up originally and at worst a more easily implemented action plan (maybe to develop the conference business) if attendance falls below expectations.

The entropy vector tells us that a too-tightly-constrained system is a high risk one; that waste and inefficiency are to be expected; that plans are a good starting place but no predictor of what will occur. Good planning and good design involve sensitivity analyses to check out the 'what if' questions and to increase tolerances.

Openness to the possibility of failure provides the freedom to see failure as feedback and a source of information that makes for future success. Business angels do not seek out entrepreneurs who have had a failure as automatic recipients of further funding. 'Hell, no,' says Russ, our East Coast friend, 'but we do ask them what they have learned from the experience and, if we are impressed, we start taking them seriously.'

The risk vector?

We have attempted in this chapter to take a look at various business risk situations from the standpoint of entropy. What can we say about such an approach? We began by looking at the start-up situation and concluded that the entrepreneur needs to build in constraints wherever possible. In other words, pursue the lowest possible entropy vector consistent with the start-up task. Inevitably a start-up is high-risk and has the potential of being a high entropy process (disorder, inefficiency, lack of structure). It is good sense to focus on what needs to be done and apply such constraints as are possible. In discussing time and entropy in Chapter 6, we plotted entropy and time on a graph and sketched a number of entropy vectors. It was apparent from this graph that a vector with a steep gradient could be achieved through either a big change in entropy or a small change in time. This is true for the entrepreneur—the rapid introduction of small changes can be as profitable as a slower launch of a huge change. Rushing the huge change raises the risks and potential profits dramatically.

When we looked earlier in this chapter at underachieving businesses, our conclusion was that the companies attempted to operate with too little entropy. Their systems, procedures and cultures all tended to over-constrain freedom, initiative and creativity. The result was that risks were minimised to the extent of preventing the companies from taking even those risks that they needed to take in order to ensure survival, let alone growth. It is as if these companies successfully started up and then put particular effort into applying constraints wherever possible. As soon as successful procedures were established they were codified and frozen, with the consequence that as the uncertainty of operation decreased (i.e. the start-up became a stable operation), the entropy vector became lower and lower, such that it fell below the path necessary for successful operation.

This necessary path corresponds to the natural entropy vector, which is controlled by the market in which your business is operating. Just as start-up companies need to look for ways of reducing entropy to contain the risks of start-up, so established companies need to look for ways of building in some freedom, some relatively high entropy vector to enable innovation and growth. There is value in having an entropy vector above the natural level, value in being inventive and imaginative. In the previous chapter we discussed the ways to stimulate creativity and to introduce these ideas and concepts into the business through innovation.

The third area of risk we looked at was where a company has a choice of ways of doing something and the management task of balancing risk, reward and efficiency. The conclusion here is that it is not simply the overall path that is important but that the order in which things are done has a significant impact on the final result. There is no simple rule to say what the order is, but it makes good sense to look at what needs to be done and to assess the risks of each step. It is likely that the step which potentially gives the greatest degree of disorder (and hence the greatest risk) is likely to be the one that, if successfully completed, gives the highest reward.

Finally, we looked at business failure and suggested that companies need to plan for failure, particularly in any new venture, not just in the sense of having a contingency plan ready if things go badly wrong but also in recognising that there will be wastage and loss of efficiency. Factors to allow for such losses must be built in at the outset. The risks of failure are high whenever we imagine that we can design out all losses and all uncertainty.

Notes and quotes

- Peter F. Drucker, *Innovation and Entrepreneurship: Practice and Principles* (Heinemann, London, 1985). He does not use the word 'entropy', but second law thinking abounds. The following is a précis of pages 122–6:

  Innovation is work; it requires knowledge. To succeed innovators must build on their strengths. Innovation is an effect in the economy and society and has to be market-driven. Innovators are conservative. They are not risk-focused, they are opportunity-focused.

  Be guided by the following principles:

  Do analyse the opportunities, look and listen, keep it simple and focused, start small, aim at leadership and don't try to be clever, diversify and splinter, try to innovate for the future.

- Mintzberg. Again, see 'Notes and quotes' at the end of Chapter 5.

- Joseph Alois Schumpeter, 1883–1950. Born in Triesch (now part of the Czech Republic) and educated at Vienna University. He began his career by practising law and then, as his reputation as an economic theorist grew, he began teaching economics, finally at Harvard. He emphasised the role of entrepreneurs in stimulating investment and innovation. He predicted that excessive government control could destroy entrepreneurialism and innovation. His best-known books are '*Die Theorie der Wirtschaftlichen Entwicklung*' ('The Theory of Economic Dynamics'), 1911, translated in 1934; *Business Cycles* (1939), *Capitalism, Socialism and Democracy* (1942) and *The History of Economic Analysis*, published posthumously in 1954.
- Parable of the talents. Any version of the Bible will do; see Matthew, Chapter 25, for the full story.
- The heart of entrepreneurship? A good starting point is the paper of the same name, written by Howard H. Stevenson and David E. Gumbert and appearing in *Harvard Business Review*, March/April, No. 2, 1985, pp. 85–94.

10

Mental Entropy

education and training • memory and analysis • efficiency, effective-ness and distinctiveness • diversity of skill and attitude • employee and team skills • science and measurement

If mental arithmetic is doing sums in your head, then what is mental entropy? If you are asked, 'What is 7 by 8?', you may well reply immediately, '56.' Or you may say, 'Just a minute, it's, er, almost got it, yep, 56.' The answer came from your memory, in one case more efficiently than the other.

Now, what if you are asked to give the approximate circumference of a circle whose diameter is 7? Again, you might give an answer immediately or after some umming and arring, but this time it is unlikely to be wholly from memory of the answer. It is likely to be the result of a calculation based on a memorised formula (circumference equals pi times diameter) and a memorised constant (pi is approximately 22 divided by 7). Thus the approximate circumference is 22 divided by 7 times 7 equals 22.

Finally, what if you are asked to give the cross-sectional dimensions of the strongest wooden beam possible that can be obtained from a perfectly cylindrical tree trunk of diameter d? Most of us would want a piece of paper for this. Most of us would need to find out the relationship between the length and the breadth of a beam that provides for maximum strength (it is unlikely that this is a formula we have retained from our school days even if we learned it there). All of us would need to apply a rigorous mathematical approach to obtain the result. Some of us would be bright enough to realise that the question needed skills that we lacked and would go off and ask an engineer.

Tell me; what's a nice beam like you doing in a log like this?

So, what is mental entropy? We use the expression to address the question of efficient and effective thinking. We pose the question as to what useful work is obtained for the energy used to operate the brain, though we do not intend to provide a quantitative answer. We will consider the value of education and training and the balance between memorising facts and the application of theory from first principles. We will touch upon the value of extending thinking beyond conventional boundaries and also address aspects of information theory. Throughout the chapter, we will be seeking to determine whether there is a particular entropy vector that helps us to steer an optimum course.

Let us begin with information! Every time we solve a problem, we seem to generate a new set of questions. In a way it is like climbing a mountain. With every ten feet climbed you see new horizons and gain new perspectives on existing ones that reshape your understanding. So, how do we make sense of all the facts that bombard us? Of all the information available in books, on the Internet, on the TV screen? Turn to page 47 of your daily or weekly paper and you will possibly find a small advert for a way to improve your memory—the more you store, the better off you will be. To an extent, yes, but the key is not 'more' but rather the employment of a logical filing system.

Simply filing information does not increase the amount you have (though it may help you not to lose some). What it does is to keep the information together in a way that gives you a better chance of using it effectively. And by filing logically, by employing some science to the task, we reduce the entropy and increase the efficiency of the process.

Richard Feynman, the celebrated Nobel laureate, started his lectures on physics by telling his students that if they were going to be physicists, they

'No, Siggins! I didn't mean you had to put your head into a filing cabinet.'

would have a lot to study, and he reminded them of two hundred years of rapidly developing knowledge. He went on to reassure them by telling them: 'In spite of the tremendous amount of work that has been done for all this time it is possible to condense the enormous mass of results to a large extent—that is, to find laws which summarize all our knowledge'. This is a good example of controlling the entropy vector. However, Professor Feynman went further by promising to provide the students with a map or outline of the relationship of physics to the rest of the sciences, the relations of the sciences to each other and the meaning of science. It is no wonder that Professor Feynman was considered one of the most brilliant teachers of physics. This approach would provide a logical filing system for his students to lodge the information that he would go on to give them. The quality of this filing system was fundamental to their ability to recall and use information; it would help them to convert information into knowledge by providing signposts and by guiding their thinking and hence ultimately (we hope) their understanding.

Memory vs analysis

OK, so maybe we don't possess Richard Feynman's brain and we haven't been fortunate enough to study under him. Yet, by employing some logical structure to our thought processes we can gain economic advantage. Well-ordered thinking (i.e. low entropy thinking) gives good results compared with woolly thinking (i.e. badly ordered or high entropy thinking).

We mentioned employing science for the task, and if we do, then we are in good company.

Aristotle was born in Thrace in Greece in 384 BC, the son of a doctor. He came to Athens at the age of 17 to join Plato's academy and stayed until Plato died, some 20 years later. He returned to Athens later in life, but not before becoming tutor to the young Alexander the Great. According to Guthrie, he was the last of the ancient and the first of the modern philosophers. As a consequence of his logic treatises and firm views that theory should follow empirical observation and logic, he stands as the grandfather of the 'scientific method'.

Scientific method is focussed on two related issues—the consistency of an argument and its truth. Aristotle's argument formula or syllogistic system has had enormous influence. (A syllogism, according to our dictionary, is 'a pattern of deductive reasoning consisting of two given or assumed propositions and a conclusion'.)

Let's have a look.

If all dogs are animals and a poodle is a dog, then a poodle is an animal. The argument is valid and we find it acceptable, though not necessarily interesting.

If all dot-com companies generate huge wealth for their founders and entropyvector.com can be formed, then Handscombe and Patterson will be wealthy. The argument is as formally valid as the earlier one but we know it isn't true. We have lived through the dot-com crash. The problem is simple, the major premise is not true and thus the conclusion is false. The dot-com experience taught us that the important thing about e-business is the business. The important thing about logic and syllogism is to make sure the basics are right.

Logic consequences arise from the combination of basic propositions and, in theory, these basic propositions together with some general classification system give us the tools to store knowledge on any subject. In practice, it usually proves impossible to store all the basic propositions and to remember how to work from them.

Don't you just groan when someone says: 'OK, we can work this out from first principles'? You know the kind of thing—it is raining, getting dark, you are on a camping trip, miles from anywhere, the person who normally sets up the tents is off sick and then this guy in the green anorak suddenly comes to life .... .

It is also pretty annoying when this approach is used in everyday life, for it is just too slow for comfort and normally we memorise some secondary information, simply because we find it convenient to have immediate access to facts and information most frequently needed in the daily exercise of our profession. If you ask a builder for a quote on roofing the garage you want him to work from a rule of thumb that tiles overlap each other by a third (or whatever the factor is) rather than sit down with his calculator and consider the rate of flow of moisture between two adjacent surfaces (with estimates of average wind velocity plus a safety factor for damage and movement).

We mentioned Richard Feynman and the value of filing logically. This is a crucial point. Although the volume of factual information has expanded continuously as civilisation has expanded, its total volume is not so important because of our increasing application of theoretical understanding. But it is an impossible task—the faster we climb the mountain, the more new horizons we see.

Yet the mountain needs to be climbed. We must find a way of coping with (and using) the information that is available. In preparing to do this, we rely heavily on schooling, education, learning and training. But what approaches are best suited to the task? Is the use of theoretical science the answer? In principle, an analytical or theoretical approach should provide a better basis for future intellectual growth but, as our school class will tell us, 'Sir, it's hard', and even the best university students look forward to descriptive courses where information is presented in a clear, digestible form. The temptation is to memorise rather than sort logically and analytically.

Training can improve both kinds of learning (memorising and analysing) but the kind of training employed needs to be based on the culture of the system. For example, Chinese and Japanese students have good memories because their tradition is one of continuous training of memory. Yet there are limits. No matter how tempting the memorising route might be, there is little chance these days of being able to memorise all the knowledge in your chosen field. So, we come back to the need for theoretical science and logical structures in addition to some memorising. In short, we need an entropy vector that leads us successfully between the unmanageable volume of facts and the unacceptable tardiness of an approach from first principles.

There is also the issue of understanding and we would argue that a key distinction of a true university is that it provides the environment and opportunity for its students to gain a solid understanding of their subjects.

Understanding means both knowing the facts and knowing the causes behind them—*Rerum Cognoscere Causas*, as our university crest puts it. ('To Discover the Causes of Things'; from Virgil's Georgics, II, 490.)

Yes, but what causes it to be four?

Thus, with some logical structure we gain information and from this we can infer, deduce, and extrapolate to other conclusions. The correct entropy vector not only takes us through existing information more effectively, it also helps us predict and manage in areas where we lack complete information.

Computers to the rescue?

But change is certain. If we have learned nothing else so far, we should have learned that. There is no escape from the second law. The balance between memory and analysis changes with increasing knowledge and with increasing technology. With the incredible growth in computer memory, in software sophistication and in artificial intelligence, it is reasonable to suspect that society is close now to when all the memorising, sorting and calculating can be done in computers and done faster, bigger, better than humans can do it. A senior communications executive said recently that his company's predictions are that the computer 'brain' which is as big and as fast as a human brain will be available in 2010. Shock, horror! It is comfortable to shut our minds to this prospect and to continue to do what we are used to, but by doing that we are allowing our entropy vector to drift too close to the low entropy axis—the controlled, constrained, ordered, systematised approach. It may be comfortable down there but we are better than electronic machines, programmed to do well-established and well-defined tasks. We can and must 'think out of the box', laterally and creatively.

We'd be lost without the computer and its ability to store and organise data for us, but it is our tool and not our master. We should not be seduced into working in a similar way and restrict ourselves to collecting, ordering, reordering and presenting information. We need to do more than this. We can be certain of chance and opportunity; our responsibility is to do the mental preparation by clear thinking and hard questioning so that we are ready.

The easy access to computer information and analysis—and the clear and professional presentation of computer printouts—make us less likely to question the appropriateness of the analysis, less likely to assess the statistical tools used in the processing of the data, less likely to test the models used in interpreting the data. All that glisters is not gold . . . .

How does society get the balance right? It needs to support basic research so as to develop new generations of computer hardware and software; it needs to provide training so its workforce can use the new technology efficiently and thus contribute to national economic competitiveness, and it needs to provide basic teaching and learning opportunities so that we are given the skills and confidence to know how to think.

Education must help lever up our entropy vector from a constrained, well-organised, computer-like approach. It must do more than provide students with the necessary tools and understanding to make sense of and organise existing information. The role model must be more challenging than a super-computer. We need to progress and, to do this, we need a more enquiring, more creative approach.

Justus von Liebig was a university professor by the time he was twenty-one, although at school he had been branded as hopelessly useless. [There is a view among some of the more reactionary of small company managing directors that 'hopelessly useless' is the qualifying feature for an academic career.] He went on to become one of the foremost chemists of his time, notably for his work on fertilisers and mineral nutrients. But the enquiring mind enquires and in 1847 he invented a process for extracting and concentrating the goodness in beef. The initial process was expensive, but an association with the entrepreneur George Giebert—who had seen, in Uruguay, a source of cheap raw material, the rotting carcasses of cattle slaughtered for their skins—led to a scaling-up of the process, a scaling-down of the cost and the formation of the Liebig Extract of Meat Company in 1865.

In 1899 the meat extract was named Oxo, and Unilever, the current owner of Liebig's company, estimate that two million Oxo cubes are used daily in the UK alone.

Most revolutionary discoveries have been made accidentally but the accidental process is tortuous. By chance, Liebig had diverted from his fertiliser work; by chance he met Giebert; by chance Giebert saw a way to make money. But Giebert was not the first person to see rotting carcasses. It wasn't simply that Giebert saw the carcasses but that, by chance, he saw them at a particular stage in his mental processes. Incidentally, those of you who continually seek to say something positive about Belgium will be pleased to note that George Giebert was a Belgian engineer.

Liebig's production line (simplified).

Accidental discovery is important but the establishment of theoretical explanation of how things work frees society from depending on accidental discovery for all developments. It provides a basis for training of the mind so that we have people receptive to and eager to find new things. Also, with a theory, there is no need to wait for accidents to happen. The theory gives us the incentive and the means to test and we can cause 'accidents' by continuously experimenting. By and large, this gives us an improved plastic rather than the invention of plastic itself, but that is a considerable gift—who would want to go back to the choice of materials available to our grandparents?

Theoretical science has given us the potential for continuous improvement. Logical, careful, thoughtful work on the shop floor produces dividends. Deviations from the expected can be investigated and corrective action taken. As a result, productivity increases. Perversely, however, as Karl Popper reminded us, the greatest strides in knowledge are made when a logically derived proposition is refuted by experiment, not when it is confirmed.

'Perversely, however'? This is an old English expression meaning 'in accordance with the second law'.

Why do we exhibit surprise when experiment refutes our propositions? The reason for this is simply that we believe our theories to be sturdier and more applicable than they are. They work for weightless beams and frictionless balls and we cannot see why they fail in real life situations.

The more we discover about the behaviour of nature, the more we discover how irrational it is. From the earliest times, humans have been challenged to understand their environment and they have attempted to develop theories to explain what they see. The risk is, we begin to convince ourselves that nature works to our 'rules' rather than believing that the rules are our best way of understanding nature. These are not new thoughts. Immanuel Kant talked about imposing laws on nature rather than inferring laws from nature. Perhaps we do this because our brains are too simple to appreciate the full complexity and diversity of nature.

Theoretical science has given us a craving for logical order and we have seen that there is value in having some logical frameworks. They help us make sense of things more easily—the office runs more efficiently, the shop floor is more productive, the market research is more effective. By organising our thought processes we are better able to spot opportunities and take advantage of them. As Louis Pasteur said (and as George Giebert and the 'Oxo' story proved): 'Chance favours only the prepared mind.'

We are back in our fantasy land if we think that we have nice, steady, stable, repeatable conditions. The normal condition is not stability: it is change. We must take care not to mark as fixed points on the mental maps recommended by Richard Feynman, those 'facts' that are subject to change. Change occurs all the time and we need to be aware of the effects. No one asked, until it was too late, 'What is different about the structural integrity of the Comet aircraft today compared with yesterday?' The human tragedy was that on 1st May 1953 Comets were making uneventful flights and on 2nd May 1953 Comet G-ALYY crashed during a severe tropical storm near Calcutta. Seven months later, on 10th January 1954, Comet G-ALYP crashed in good weather near the island of Elba at 0951 after leaving Rome at 0931. Four months after this second crash, on

8th April 1954, another Comet left Rome for Cairo and, after reporting its estimated time of arrival at 1905, was never heard from again.

The Comet aircraft went into service with British Overseas Airways Corporation (BOAC) in May 1952. Powered by four de Havilland Ghost turbo-jet engines, it was designed to cruise at 32,000 feet, compared with the 17,000 feet of existing civil aircraft, which used turbo-prop engines. So, the Comet represented a big step change in aircraft technology. A large proportion of G-ALYY was recovered and the failure traced to a crack that had started from the corner of a window in the cabin roof. Comets G-ALYP and G-ALYY had flown 1290 and 900 flights respectively, and so the conclusion was drawn that in a relatively small number of cycles a fatigue crack had grown long enough to cause a fast fracture of the metal fuselage.

Of course, we now know much more about metal fatigue and aeroplane design, but the change in the performance of metals after a few million vibration cycles took innocent lives and destroyed de Haviland's leading position in its industry sector.

In passing, we should remember that we must take care not to consider change to be just change. Aristotle classically analysed change into various forms, but a trip to the ice-cream counter of our local store will reveal bigger and smaller versions of what we saw last year (change in quantity) and different flavours, shapes and textures (change in quality). We can note, too, that the ice-cream van that pulls up across the street means that we need not visit the store at all (change in place). As ever, we need to understand clearly what we mean by the words we use. The expression 'the management of change' might tempt us into thinking that change was a single entity. It is not and we stand a good chance of increasing the disorder if in attempting to manage change we consider only one of its dimensions.

Zeno's paradox

And if we stick with the ancient Greeks for a moment, we can enjoy one of Zeno's paradoxes. Consider an arrow shot from the firing line towards the target. It leaves the bow and later hits the target, but consider it for a moment in its flight. At a particular moment, it is at a particular place in the air, somewhere between the bow and the target. And if it is at a place, then it must be at rest there.

But if the arrow is at rest, then how does it continue on its journey because things do not move from rest on their own?

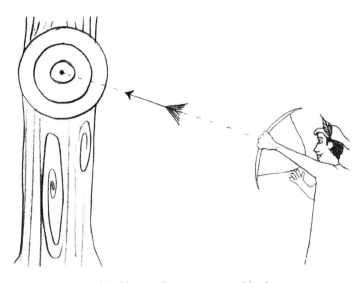

Ye olde spot the arrow competition?

The complication that this paradox relies on is that if one refers only to an instant of time it is impossible to distinguish between rest and motion. There is a difference between being in a place and moving through a place, but restricted logical analysis does not allow that difference and hence the paradox and confusion. It is a paradox worth remembering, for the second law dictates that we are moving through rather than being at.

If we let ourselves be seduced by the importance of measurement, then we risk losing touch with the real object. One of us spent some time in his early career in the control room of a continuous glass fibre making plant. The control room, then with those wonderful circular charts and ink-spitting pens, was fed information from the raw material batch feeder, from the furnace itself and from the forehearths—very carefully controlled troughs that prepared the glass prior to its being pulled through fine orifices to form fibres. With all those charts, instruments and information, was there any need to go out onto the hot dusty plant? One of the favourite stories during the early morning hours of a long shift was how, on one distant occasion, the control room engineers spent an hour trying everything to get the forehearth temperatures back to normal but to no avail. So, in desperation, at a little after 2 a.m., they called out the furnace engineer. None too pleased to have been called out, he arrived on site, donned his helmet and 'walked' the furnace. Somehow the lagging on one of the air ducts had had oil spilt on it and had caught fire. This new source of heat was not controllable from within the control room and created an abnormal reading on the nearest thermocouple. All the changes made in the control room affected other variables and caused other deviations from the required conditions. The furnace engineer put the fire out, reset the controls to normal and went back home.

In this chapter, we have looked at mental entropy and advocated an entropy vector that steers a course between the disorder of unmanaged facts and the constraints of pure theory, logic and methodology. The argument is for a vector that recognises both sides of its path. Major discoveries do occur by accident and a great deal of learning is possible in schools, in higher education and in continuing professional development by encouraging experimentation and thinking 'outside the box'. However, the successful vector is one that also takes in some basic logical rules, some grounding in science and measurement and some intellectual frameworks such that our minds are prepared for serendipity and we are able to make continuous improvements—to our knowledge and to our activities—by logical extrapolation from what we know.

Although science is powerful, we should not steer our course too close to it. Galileo Galilei was born in Pisa, Italy, in 1564 and became a professor of mathematics there at the age of 25. His experiments, developments and observations revolutionised science. Science was about measurement and his arguments in favour of the earth and other planets being in motion around the sun, based on his measurements with his telescope, got him into some serious trouble with the Church authorities. There is little doubt, however, that his enormous scientific advances, for example in the field of astronomy, were the result of meticulous measurement.

The danger is in taking the comment 'science is measurement' and applying it broadly. Scientific theories are particularly useful as they are grounded in measurement, which means they can be tested and we can be confident of their reproducibility. They involve discrete, distinct concepts amenable to logical shifting. Wherever they can be applied they give insight and clear understanding, but they have limited application. Indeed, Karl Popper argued that there is a very clear distinction between scientific theories and non-scientific ones. He suggested that a scientific theory is not one which explains everything that can possibly happen. On the contrary, he claims that it rules out most of what could possibly happen and is therefore ruled out itself if what it rules out does happen. According to Popper, 'A scientific theory places itself permanently at risk.' The ability to be falsified, to be proved wrong because what it says should happen doesn't, is the criterion of demarcation between science and non-science. Only if it is testable is it scientific.

Thus some science helps, but obsession is limiting. We keep on measuring intelligence by IQ but we do not know exactly what is being measured. More recently, there has been an increasing emphasis on EI (emotional intelligence), with a suggested set of qualitative indicators to enable us to believe there is a basis for its measurement. Daniel Goleman suggests that 'of the two EI adds far more to the qualities that make us more fully human' and also points out the lack of a 'single paper and pencil test' to give us the EI score.

Managers talk of calculated risk, but rarely on the basis of having done a calculation, and even if they have, would we know how to check their calculation? The implication is that if we can be coaxed into believing that things can be measured, then, because science is measurement, the 'thing' must be grounded in science and be 'right'. This is fool's gold. The danger is that we end up believing either that measurement is everything or that because we can measure something we actually understand what is going on.

On the other hand, simply introducing 'non-science' to balance the approach and to increase the value of the entropy vector is not to be recommended. As Popper observed, the demarcation between science and non-science is not the same as that between sense and nonsense. The challenge is to choose carefully. We have spoken earlier about the difference between woolly and creative thinking. Both introduce entropy into a process but they are not synonymous. If we add a creative person to our logical, scientific and methodological team, then we stand a chance of progress and improvement. If we choose woolliness, then at best we get the status quo if our initial team is capable of defending its systems, but more likely we get deterioration and decline.

Closing time

So, what is mental entropy? We conclude by asking the same question that we asked at the beginning of the chapter. We used the expression to address the question of efficient and effective thinking and mental entropy can be seen to be a measure of wasteful brain-work. In developing our thinking here, we have seen that to arrive at a valuable vector for mental entropy—where mental outputs are efficient yet not rigidly fixed—a number of factors need to apply.

One needs education to provide students with the necessary tools and understanding to make sense and organise existing information and to encourage creativity and enquiry. Training is required to improve both kinds of learning (memorising and analysing) and to give practice in extending thinking beyond conventional boundaries. A scientific approach is important to enable a logical and systematic filing of information, as well as a non-science element to give team work and motivation. This is asking a lot of a single person but such gems exist.

More broadly, it gives a steer to those who are responsible for developing and managing teams, for in assembling a team there is a need to incorporate diverse skills and attitudes to achieve the desired cumulative mental entropy. Variety is important, but the selection must not be random, for this would add an unwanted and unnecessary extra source of entropy. Mental processes are capable of generating more than enough without such assistance!

Notes and quotes

- For those still troubled by the beam question ... the answer is that the height and breadth need to be in the ratio of one to the square root of two.
- How to select a team? Much has been written on this and of the many tools available, the 'self-perception inventory' of Raymond Meredith Belbin is worth attention. For further reading see: R.M. Belbin, *Team Roles at Work* (Butterworth–Heinemann, Oxford, 1993).
- Nicholas Georgescu-Roegen, *The Entropy Law and the Economic Process* (Harvard University Press, Cambridge (Mass.) and Oxford University Press, 1971). Once more, we have introduced a number of ideas from this book and have followed up on several of his references.
- Karl R. Popper, *The Logic of Scientific Discovery* (Routledge, London, 1995). This is a translation of the original 1934 work ('*Logik der Forschung*') and, according to the dust cover, is 'one of the most important documents of the twentieth century'. Karl Popper was born in Vienna in 1902 and is regarded by many as the greatest philosopher of science that there has ever been. An excellent introduction to his work is provided by Bryan Magee in *Popper* (Fontana Modern Masters, Fontana/Collins, London, 1973).
- 'All that glisters is not gold. Often have you heard that told'—William Shakespeare, *Merchant of Venice*, Act II, Scene VII, and, you will recall, the sad outcome for the Prince of Morocco, who failed to win the hand of Portia because of his enchantment with gold.
- Richard P. Feynman has been described as an American cultural icon. In 1965 he shared the Nobel Prize in Physics with Sin-Itero Tomanaga and Julian Schwinger for his work on quantum electrodynamics. At the California Institute of Technology, from 1961 to 1963, he delivered a series of lectures that have changed the way physics is taught

around the world. *Lectures on Physics* was published and the most accessible lectures were reproduced in *Six Easy Pieces*, by Richard Feynman (Addison-Wesley Reading, Mass., 1996). Some of the ideas mentioned in this chapter can be found in the first lecture.

- 'The error of the mediocre person entangles the threads and curbs advancement .... . Not so Liebig. When he erred, he had the courage and distinctness of the creative error'—Fritz Haber, in his chapter 'Justus von Liebig, 1803–1873', pp. 535–49, in *Great Chemists*, edited by Eduard Farber (Interscience, New York & London, 1964).

- A detailed analysis of the Comet disaster can be found in *Engineering Materials 3: Materials Failure Analysis*, by D.R.H. Jones (Pergamon, Oxford, 1993); and in 'Fatigue and the Comet Disasters', by T. Bishop, in *Source Book in Failure Analysis* (American Society for Metals, 1974), p. 204.

- Louis Pasteur's observations that 'Chance favours the prepared mind' ('*Le hasard favorse l'esprit prepare*') evolved from his observation of experiments. He saw that there was an element of chance but also an element of preparation, and whilst preparation does not guarantee creativity, it does increase probability.

- Zeno's paradox? 'An object is at rest when it occupies a space equal to its own dimensions. An arrow in flight occupies at any given moment a space equal to its own dimensions. Therefore an arrow in flight is at rest.' This approach divides time and space into infinitesimal increments, which implies that time is composed of instants for which the arrow is at rest. G.S. Kirk and J.E. Raven, *The Presocratic Philosophers* (Cambridge University Press, 1964), pp. 294–5.

- For more on Aristotle, check out W.K.C. Guthrie, *A History of Greek Philosophy, Vol. VI: Aristotle—An Encounter* (Cambridge University Press, 1981).

- The expression 'emotional intelligence' was brought to many people's attention by Daniel Goleman's book of the same name, published by Bloomsbury (London) in 1996. For those looking for the basic definition of emotional intelligence, try the paper where the model was first proposed: 'Emotional Intelligence', Peter Salovey and John D. Mayer, in *Imagination, Cognition and Personality*, 9, 1990, pp. 185–211.

11

Entropy Trade-offs

power packs and technology vectors • labour market, incentives and equilibrium • improbable happenings

Change forces choice; choice causes change. In this chapter, we shall explore the choices and consequences of entropy change. Aubrey Wilson tells us that 'the primary aim of management is to bring about change', yet this is in the context of a universe that is constantly changing. Just what change is for the good and what are the consequences? This is a tough question. Most organisations are busy trying to manage the natural entropy of their systems (and prevent a progression to disorder) at the same time as attempting to introduce new changes that fit their objectives. There will be trade-offs between the work done and the work left undone; trade-offs between energy (or other resources) committed and energy saved and trade-offs between the types of entropy generated in the system. Selecting the best entropy vector requires a working knowledge of the trade-offs involved. Where shall we begin?

We have seen in earlier chapters that with effort it is possible to reduce the entropy gain in a process. We considered the cooling of a slab of iron by immersing it in a single cold bath (high entropy process) or by cooling it in a succession of baths with decreasing temperatures (low entropy process). The slab of iron ends up at the same temperature in both cases but there is a trade-off between entropy gain, time taken and work done.

Similarly, when free energy or exergy is used to create work—for example, coal being burned to produce steam to drive an engine—the amount of work that can be done from a given unit of exergy resource increases with increasing efficiency of the system. There is, of course, a corresponding decrease in entropy gain. Conversely, a process with a high entropy gain produces relatively little work.

However, there is a further trade-off that we should consider. Not only is there the very straightforward balance between work and entropy but also something rather less obvious. We have seen above, in the example of the slab of iron, that by changing the process, the efficiency and hence the entropy change can be modified. Changing a process introduces new options and new constraints. In short, new opportunities for entropy trade-offs.

Mobile power packs

We have talked of steam engines, so let us continue with them to explore what kind of trade-offs can be involved as one changes a process. We should start at the beginning and go back two hundred years to Thomas Savery and Thomas Newcomen, at the turn of the eighteenth century. Savery lived in Cornwall and Newcomen was an ironmonger in Dartmouth; both were involved in the mining industry.

Looking back, one can identify as a driving force for invention, the objective of making mining an easier, safer and more profitable activity. The three overriding problems were poor air, a tendency to flood and the difficulty of raising the ore to the surface. Manually operated bellows were known and in use but they had limited effect. Something altogether more powerful was required to move air, to pump water and to lift ore. Savery and then, more effectively, Newcomen came up with the answer— the steam engine. A cumbersome, slow, inefficient beam engine, difficult to control and, once set up, best not moved. Nonetheless, this was a major innovation and it was used extensively for pumping water from coalmines.

It is worth looking at Newcomen's engine for a minute. We have discussed in earlier chapters the idea of a technology trajectory, and the Newcomen engine will occupy a low point on the 'engine trajectory'. With hindsight, the first steps on that trajectory look crude. Newcomen's device had a vertical cylinder and a piston that was counterweighted. Low pressure steam was allowed to enter the bottom of the cylinder and the effect of this, together with the counterweight, caused the piston to move to the top of the cylinder. There, a valve opened automatically and a jet of cold water sprayed into the cylinder, condensing the steam and permitting atmospheric pressure to force the piston back down to the bottom of the cylinder. A rod attached to the arm of the pivoted beam that connected piston and counterweight moved up and down as the piston moved, actuating a pump.

It took the inspiration of other inventors, first James Watt and then Richard Trevithick, to modify the steam engine so that it had the efficiency, control and power-to-weight ratio that permitted it to become the prime mover in locomotion. The iron horse had been born. Transport was revolutionised with the railways, and the easier control and lower mass of the engine spelt the demise of water power in industry. It also paved the way for the rapid growth of factories and industrial development, first in England and then throughout the developing world.

So, just what did Watt do and where was the trade-off, for the analysis so far has shown an endless stream of benefits? James Watt was an instrument maker and repairman at the University of Glasgow. When he was asked to repair a model of a Newcomen engine, he realised that he could make it more efficient. Watt's first important development was the design of an engine that incorporated a separate condensing chamber for the steam. This engine, patented in 1769, greatly increased the economy of the Newcomen machine by avoiding the waste of steam required for the heating and cooling of the engine cylinder. In Watt's engine, the cylinder was insulated and remained at steam temperature. Watt also used higher pressure steam such that it was the steam pressure and not atmospheric pressure that drove the piston and as a consequence enabled greater power. Watt also developed a way for the reciprocating pistons to drive a flywheel and a way for steam to be admitted at both ends of the cylinder to drive the piston even faster. He also introduced throttle valves to control speed and, notably, a governor in order to maintain automatically a constant speed of operation.

Watt's impact was enormous but it was Richard Trevithick, a Cornish blacksmith, who devised the use of non-condensing engines using high pressure steam and Trevithick used such an engine to power the first railway locomotive ever made. To quote Jacob Bronowski, 'He turned the steam engine into a mobile power pack.'

Watt's innovations increased the efficiency of the process. The separate condenser enabled more useful work to be obtained for each shovelful of coal and, correspondingly, the entropy gain of the process was reduced. The governor automatically made the process more ordered and less prone to slipping away from the desired working range. This gave his engine more potential to do work and increased its range of applications.

But what of the further trade-off that we discussed earlier? So far, we have identified only the straightforward balance between work and entropy. The answer is in the design. Watt was able to make the improvements

because he studied the properties of steam in order to understand how best to use it. The consequence of this was a higher degree of sophistication in the design and manufacture of the engine. There was an increase in efficiency and a decrease in entropy production but associated with this decrease was the requirement to increase the skill and understanding of those involved in its manufacture and use. Increasingly, the development of the steam engine required precision engineering, in particular to prevent the high pressure steam from escaping between the piston and the cylinder. When Watt was granted his patent in 1769, no one could manufacture a cylinder to a high enough tolerance. It wasn't until 1776, when a Frenchman, Brigadier de la Houlière and the Wilkinson brothers between them developed a machine that could accurately bore a cylinder, that the true value of Watt's invention could be realised.

Technology trajectories

The trade-off—higher efficiency but at the expense of higher skill input—is a common entropy trade-off. It is the reason why companies and countries that wish to keep ahead of the rest on any given technology trajectory need to make the necessary investments in education and training. Higher efficiency implies lower entropy production but you only get a reduction in entropy in a closely defined area. If you take into account all relevant activities, then, overall, entropy continues to increase. The second law will not go away.

In Chapter 8, we introduced the idea of technopy and drew a technopy curve. It might be useful to redraw it here to look at the engine developments that we have just discussed. The figure below shows entropy (or technopy) plotted against time. The natural entropy or technology level is constantly increasing. James Watt produced a significant advance in the engine technology and gave himself a technology trajectory above the natural one. The consequence was the widespread use of his engines, together with fame that has lasted until today. A company that steadfastly stuck to manufacturing his engines would by now have fallen way below the natural entropy line and would only survive with major subsidies from sentimental benefactors. Interestingly, sixty years before Watt's invention Thomas Savery had invented a pumping engine which frequently failed because the metal joints would split open due to the solder melting. Perhaps Savery's technology trajectory was too ambitious—certainly, his pumping engine did not make the mark of Watt's.

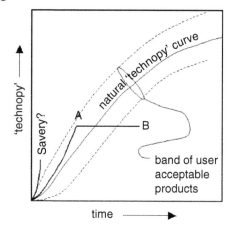

A — Watt produced a significant advance to get
    ahead of the natural curve
B — a company that has stuck steadfastly to Watt's
    design will now be too far behind the natural
    curve to operate commercially

Some of the improvements that Watt introduced, such as the device called a governor, made the steam engine easier to control. We might say that he introduced more flexible working arrangements but the entropy was reduced and we normally expect reductions in entropy to be associated with less, not more, flexibility! There seems to be a paradox here: more flexible working arrangements at the same time as a less flexible, more controlled process. We can resolve this in two ways. First, and this is sound management practice, check carefully to see what the words mean. The steam engine became more 'flexible' in that it could be used for a wider range of duties in a wider range of conditions. This greater flexibility in use was achieved by constraining the actual speed of the piston. Watt's design had more potential to do work. The potential to do useful work is a form of exergy and what we have here is a phenomenon that we have met already—'exergy up and entropy down in a local pocket'. We are back to looking at entropy inside and outside of tightly defined boundaries.

The second way of considering this is related. The issue is not entropy but the entropy vector. We cannot choose to reduce the entropy of an overall system—the second law just will not permit us no matter how hard we try. The steam engine and its surroundings must experience an increase in entropy. Only in the land of perpetual motion machines and frictionless bearings will this not occur and for better or worse we do not live there. All we can do is choose where entropy gains are restricted and the skill at doing this is a skill worth acquiring, for there are gains in efficiency and economy to be had.

Damn braces. Bless relaxes.
(*William Blake, 1757–1827*)

So, let us move on. As Blake rather pithily puts it, we should be resentful of restrictions (braces) and try to get rid of them whilst welcoming and praising the removal of constraints (relaxes). If a steam engine that exhibits flexibility is more effective than one that doesn't, maybe companies that exhibit flexibility will be more effective too.

There is a glimpse of truth here, which goes some way to explaining why some small firms are successful. Normally, small companies are more flexible and have more relaxed working arrangements. This might give them a good starting point but it would be unwise to go on from this to say that a small organisation has an automatic competitive advantage, or indeed that because it has flexibility it automatically has appropriate control. It too needs a governor; in fact, it needs two. It needs a governor in the sense of someone in charge and a governor in the Watt sense of a system to ensure feedback. A Watt-type governor will provide the process control that is required to ensure that the whole operation has the necessary flexibility to operate and prosper. Questions about availability of finance and breadth of management skill will quickly qualify just how flexible the company is and how successful it will be. Small may be beautiful but effective control and competitive advantage are more important.

So let us be more specific and look again at the point made earlier, namely that Watt introduced more flexible working arrangements. Let us put on one-side general questions of flexibility and ask: To what extent do a company's employment arrangements make the company easier to control?

There are indeed economic arguments which claim that flexible working arrangements (a flexible labour market in economicspeak) do provide for easier control and as a consequence a healthier economy and higher employment level.

The Economist, in February 1999, reviewed some recent research under the heading 'Working Man's Burden'. The article was based on a paper (unpublished at the time of the *Economist* review) by Rafael Di Tella of Harvard University and Robert MacCulloch of the University of Bonn. Di Tella and MacCulloch carried out a study tracking 21 countries over 7 years to 1990 and interviewing over 1000 companies. They set out to ask company managers to gauge how flexible their enterprises were in terms of making adjustments to job security and of compensation standards in order to deal with 'economic realities'. In simple terms, the question was: How easy is it for you to shed staff when the going gets tough? Managers were asked to give a reply on a scale of 0 to 100. The authors reached the following conclusions. First, that labour market flexibility does increase employment, and they suggested from their findings that if for example France's labour market had been as flexible as that of the United States then its rates of employment would have been around 25% higher (leading to higher output and higher gross domestic product per head).

They also drew conclusions about unemployment, though they accepted that it was a more complicated issue. However, their analysis of the results indicates that increased flexibility causes unemployment to fall, and they suggested that if France had been as flexible as the United States then its unemployment rate would have halved. *The Economist* reproduced a table indicating that Spain, with an average unemployment level of 19%, had a flexibility score of 30 whilst Switzerland, with an average unemployment level of 2%, had a flexibility score of 60. In short, the article concluded that what right wing politicians say about labour market flexibility appears to be true.

This is a nice example of academic research, for it is interesting enough to cause a debate. It permits radio pundits and politicians to argue that evidence exists that shorter-term contracts for staff lead to greater efficiency and greater employment for a national economy. Other pundits, of course, will suggest that this is possible only at a nationally lower average wage rate.

Purists would argue, as on the radio in the week of the *Economist* article, that the statistics are poor and that, in reality, the only correlation for unemployment is housing. They would point to Spain, which has high home ownership and high unemployment, and to Switzerland, which has both low home ownership and low unemployment.

Does this mean that tackling the housing market will reduce employment? Well, perhaps not. If we listen carefully to the purists, we will note that they said correlation, but did not say causal correlation.

As with many economic arguments, a straight comparison of short or long term contracts is difficult to make. There are political issues and temporal ones. In the space of a four-year term of office a political decision in favour of short-termism can give good results, or at least good for the political prospects of that party. As we all know, not everything is short-term. There are long-term issues such as loyalty and these will have an adverse effect in companies and countries that opt for short-termism.

Can an entropy analysis help us to make sense of this? After all, a flexible labour market is a more disordered system than the one where everybody has well-defined and permanent contracts.

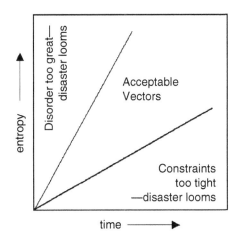

A movement from low entropy to high entropy is a move in the natural direction—we recall Clausius telling us that energy is constant but that entropy is increasing. So, if we arrange things so that there is an accelerated move from low to high disorder—in other words, an arrangement where disorder is created at faster than a natural rate (i.e. causing the high entropy condition to exist)—then we might expect something in exchange. We have learned already from Georgescu-Roegen that the economic process is associated with an increase in entropy and that the value we get from it is a 'net improvement in enjoyment of life'. So, why not increase the rate of entropy creation and get even more enjoyment of life? Those in favour of short-term contracts might argue that the greater national employment and hence a potentially higher standard of living did exactly that.

But in our excitement of creating additional entropy, have we introduced some unwanted disorder? Indeed we have, for there are costs other than the costs of implementing the arrangement. People are involved and there are psychological and social costs. The effects of less stable conditions can be identified as anxiety, worries and stress. These are human, not physical, outcomes. There are 'costs' here outside the straightforward equation. Again, how you define the system makes a difference. There are entropy trade-offs that need to be considered.

In a straightforward physical process—say, the burning of oil—we can measure heat output and temperature changes, even estimate the changes in entropy, but as far as we know, the individual atoms and molecules in the barrel of oil are unconcerned. They show no signs of anxiety—their only interest, or so it seems, is in the thermodynamic imperative of finding the lowest exergy position. If we can assume that humans behave similarly, then a drive to higher entropy in an economic process will have a concurrent higher 'enjoyment of life' factor.

Companies, however, are made up of people, and people do not behave like atoms. More and more of the value of a company results from the intellectual activity of its people and, as Charles Handy has pointed out, perhaps we should wean ourselves off the concept of a company being property and think of it as a community. Staff should be encouraged to think of themselves as belonging to a company and not of a company belonging to someone else. Managers should think of their staff as part of their asset base and not as consumables.

Incidentally, the comment about atoms finding their most thermodynamically stable position is interesting. In a sense that is what successful companies do—they find the position in a market where they can most effectively operate. Michael Porter expressed this eloquently back in his 1980 book *Competitive Strategy* when he said: 'The goal of competitive strategy for a business unit in an industry is to find a position in the industry where the company can best defend itself against the competitive forces or can influence them in its favour.'

We have argued throughout this book that the key management issue is the choice of the entropy vector. The definition of the system is crucial. If the system is the global market in which your organisation is operating, then arranging very-short-term contracts for all your staff is likely to lead to a very high turnover of staff and great disorder in the skill base of your organisation. This corresponds to a high entropy path and, if it is too high, your organisation will fail. The other extreme is lifetime golden handcuffs for all your employees. This is excessive constraint that stifles development of the company and the danger is that the entropy path is so low that your company lags badly behind in terms of enterprise and development. Again, the outcome will be failure. The path of success is somewhere in between, preferably just ahead of the natural entropy vector, the vector in your particular global market.

In the absence of dogma, one must fall back on good sense and analysis. Thomas Stewart, in his book *Intellectual Capital*, distinguishes between those staff who are easy to replace and do relatively low-value-added work and those who are difficult to replace and provide high value addition. Whilst a short-term employment approach to the former creates few problems—one advertisement in the local paper is likely to get a dozen suitable applicants—rather more care needs to be taken with the second group. Stewart argues strongly that such staff represent intellectual assets that need nurturing, protecting, securing and maintaining. Short-term contracts seem wholly inappropriate here and management effort to do even more than permanent employment contracts would be good. Stewart draws our attention to Microsoft, where, in large measure, Gates and Allen took their company public in 1986 in order to give their employees a financial incentive to keep their assets working for Microsoft rather than take them elsewhere.

Let us return to the definition of the system for a moment, and having considered it from the point of view of the organization, now look at it from the point of view of the individual. Golden handcuffs might initially seem attractive but they are constraining and stop you exploiting new opportunities. Too often, there is no incentive to do better, no incentive for the company to promote you. You are going to stand still while everyone in your neighbourhood is advancing and improving themselves. We can look at this on a personal entropy–time chart. The golden handcuff approach is path D. Iron handcuffs or shackles, i.e. slavery and heavy constraint, are path E, pointing downwards and even more undesirable. Queuing at the dock gates each day for work is at the other extreme, path A. This is completely unconstrained but ultimately inhibits personal advancement and enjoyment. So, once again, you need to aim just above the natural entropy to gain an advantage. People who do well in their careers are usually flexible; they are prepared to move from company to company and from city to city if necessary but also to stay long enough to have an impact, thus making themselves attractive to their next employer.

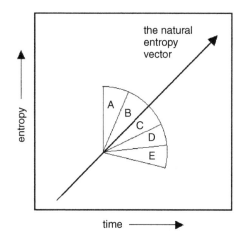

A—unconstrained and unemployed
B—movers and shakers
C—coasters and followers
D—locked-in (golden handcuffs)
E—locked-up (iron handcuffs)

Acceptable diversity of wealth?

A society in which everyone is paid the same and owns the same amount of assets would be boring due to the lack of diversity, and also highly constrained. Such a society is a theoretical ideal, though the East European countries of the 1950s to mid-1980s are examples of where this type of economic philosophy was applied. Any visitor to those countries in that period would see and feel immediately how constrained life was. When the constraint is released, movement towards the equilibrium state immediately begins and, as with any sudden removal of constraint, the movement is turbulent. The equilibrium state is that of maximum entropy, with a disordered or random distribution of wealth.

Many of the Eastern bloc countries are encountering rather more disorder than they would like. The reason is that the entropy vector is too steep. The 'unconstrained' Western way of life is not without its constraints—economic rules, laws, procedures, systems; in short, a cultural web that defines our paradigm—the way we do things in the West. Until the Eastern bloc countries establish such a framework for economic activity, their trade-off of communism for capitalism will be less satisfactory than they will have dreamt.

The capitalist system creates a diversity of possession, wealth and control systems which together provide incentives to the have-nots and disincentives to the haves. Generally, individuals attempt to improve and advance themselves and their families. However, amongst the haves the second half of the saying 'From rags to riches and back again in three generations' comes true surprisingly often. The incentives disappear for the rich, the entropy vector gets lowered below the natural one and poverty looms. On the other hand, the poor (the 'rags' at the start of the saying) have little or nothing to lose and so high entropy vectors are risked—with, sometimes, outstanding results.

Of course, if the disparities between the haves and the have-nots is too great, there is room for social discontent and disenfranchisement. The have-nots are tempted to set a particularly steep entropy vector that disregards the constraints of law and order. Crime and anarchy can result. So, again, a trade-off or balance is necessary. The unfettered, unconstrained economics of the free world that provides for growth and prosperity can function effectively only if it is fettered and constrained. Flexible working arrangements need control systems.

The *Economist* report referred to earlier in this chapter indicated that it would be possible to compute the additional employees which could result if the French economy was made as flexible as the economy of the United States. What about the reverse direction? To reduce the flexibility of the United States to that of France would be a reduction in entropy and therefore we might expect a reduction in the enjoyment of life. The article implies that there would be a cost in terms of employment and there would certainly be a requirement for an expenditure of energy (if only the food to keep the people alive who are doing the conversion; the trees to produce the paper; the oil/coal to produce the energy...). Using natural resources to ensure a reduction in the enjoyment of life looks a bad bet.

We can set the boundaries, as we have above. On the one hand, we can consider that using natural resources to ensure a reduction in the enjoyment of life looks a bad bet, and on the other, that there is some potential value if we create disorder at faster than a natural rate to get a net enjoyment of life. But where do we steer in between these extremes, for we would probably also agree that some constraints in society are essential and too much disorder is unpleasant? There is also the stark and moralistic environmentalist view that too high an interest in short term gains and excessive 'enjoyment of life' ensures the absence of long term enjoyment as a consequence of pollution and depletion of natural resources. We have a responsibility to the future but there are also day-to-day management issues. The free, unconstrained nature of short term contracts enables higher national employment but should be balanced by some structure to minimise the stress and anxiety of the workforce.

The choice is not between black and white but in the selection of the most effective grey. It is also a tortuous course. Introducing some systematisation into a company results in a reduction of entropy but, as we considered earlier, controlling some processes provides for greater flexibility overall. There is no simple rule in choosing the right entropy vector but you need to recognise that there is one and, like a good sea captain, you have to judge the course by shrewd analysis of the variables that present themselves.

Making the improbable happen

The economic research referred to above may give some macro insight but, at the micro level, at the level of each company, a rather more delicate tool is needed. At a macro level, our statistics colleagues will tell us that if you give enough chimps enough alphabet blocks and enough time, then they will produce the complete works of William Shakespeare. In practice, we tend to ignore such outcomes. In Chapter 3, three-year-old Isobel typed 154 apparently random letters using the same 27 keys used to write the preceding sentence, but the probability of her writing the same sentence is about 1 in 3 times 10 to the power of 220, or 3 with 220 noughts after it (1/27 multiplied by itself 154 times). It is possible but not probable and we cannot rely on this approach providing for our literary needs. It is not a business proposition.

So, each company needs to make its own judgements and its own entropy balances. On a national level there may be evidence to indicate that flexible labour arrangements (i.e. relatively high entropy arrangements) lead to higher employment, but at a local level companies need to compensate for this 'extra entropy' by arrangements to ensure that at least their key staff feel secure and are motivated to be loyal. Companies cannot assume that high entropy is always good. Some systematisation (i.e. reductions in entropy) of procedures and practices is likely to provide increases in efficiency and with that some potential increase in profit to the benefit of all.

Systematisation allows dangerously high entropy vectors to be modified to ones closer to the natural curve. This looks desirable, yet systems need designing and managing and thus the reduced entropy is sustainable only at the cost of a higher intellectual or skill input. If you do not have the skill to operate them properly, systems become straightjackets and the result is a move through the path of the natural vector to one that is dangerously below it.

In short, some entropy gains are good, others are not, and in either case there are other issues—trade-offs—that need considering. Remember: 'you can't have something for nothing' and 'you can't have it just anyway you like it'. The best course is not necessarily the easiest to steer, but it is worth developing the skills and understanding to attempt it, for one thing is certain. All other courses are worse.

Natural disorder is cost-free! Consider leaves swept up in a pile in your front garden as you clean up after summer and prepare for winter. It may begin as a neat pile but the wind, the exhaust from passing cars and other waste or spurious energies will cause it to become more disordered. There is no intended or desirable output except by chance. We may hope that our leaves will blow into the doorway of our least favourite neighbour, but probably they will not. On the other hand, a forced entropy change has a cost involved and will have a desired output. And this is true in both directions; there will be exergy costs required to decrease entropy (for example, effort from you to keep the leaves in some kind of order) and exergy costs to increase entropy in a controlled and accelerated direction. We could accelerate the entropy change by bringing in one of those giant fans used on film sets to generate a gale. The leaves would be distributed much more quickly, but at a cost.

Ancient and mega

You can have flexibility, but at a price. In short, flexibility costs. Sometimes the costs are straightforward; the open return airline ticket costs more than the fixed term package. Sometimes the costs are less obvious.

In the United Kingdom, one of the fastest-growing businesses over the last half century and particularly over the last twenty years has been that of higher education. Participation rates have gone up by a factor of five or more and access has never been wider. The growth is due to expansion of existing universities, creation of new ones (often from former colleges of further education) and creation of new, mega-universities with wholly new forms of teaching.

The expression 'mega-university' was used by Sir John Daniel, Vice-Chancellor of the UK's Open University, at the 12th International Meeting of University Administrators, in Edinburgh, September 1999. He was using it to encompass the Open University and similar organisations where the student population (150,000 in the case of the OU) is almost a factor of ten greater than typical domestic university student populations and where the students study from their home locations rather than from a university campus. He was talking about an entropy trade-off, though he did not put it that way. Not knowing you are talking about entropy is part of the disorder that is inevitable whenever entropy is involved.

The theme of his address was that the flexibility of traditional lecturer-based teaching is being replaced by newer forms, which may be better but are less flexible and demand greater support from the administrative staff of a university. He described the traditional form of teaching as one where the individual academic plans the curriculum, where the same person organises the learning resources and teaches the course and where finally he or she sets and marks the assessments (sometimes with central and external assistance).

The system, he concluded, was a very robust one. Individual academics are flexible and resourceful and can readily adapt if something goes wrong. They can rearrange classes if successive lessons are cancelled through bad weather; they can juggle with exam questions so that if parts of courses are missed out, the questions set are focused on the material taught; they can adjust marks if the overall performance is poor; they can find a different room if the planned one is unavailable; they can tweak the material during the course of the lectures to integrate any new reality (e.g. the Berlin wall comes down, the South-east Asian economy hiccups, a new subatomic particle is discovered).

In a traditional university, teaching is carried out with very little involvement of university administrators and with little demand on their time. Put very simply, provided the administrators register the students, collect their fees, pay the staff, keep the lecture rooms clean and warm, the teaching and learning will occur.

The situation is very different in the newer mega-universities, where they operate a system of distance learning and distance education in which they seek to ensure greater access, equal quality and reduced cost. This is a hard task. The evidence is that they are achieving it and doing so by ensuring teaching specialisation amongst the academic staff, teamwork between academic and administrative staff, and effective project management. Sir John Daniel suggests that the key innovation of Walter Perry (founding VC of the Open University in the UK in 1969) was the 'course team', with the consequence that on a traditional campus the teacher teaches, whereas in distance learning the university teaches.

The new system relies on the latest information and communications technologies but Sir John argues that it is the soft technologies of processes, approaches, sets of rules and models of organisation that are the most important. To cope with technology changes the university needs a sound framework for soft technologies to ensure it employs the hard technologies effectively.

Can we identify the trade-off? We have noted that more students from wider catchments can be taught at equivalent quality and lower cost. We know from our paraphrase of the first law of thermodynamics that 'you can't have something for nothing' and we might point to the investment in computers and communications. This would be too easy and it is a common error to believe that the introduction of faster, cleverer technology will solve problems. We must remember the second law, which we paraphrased as 'you can't have it anyway you like'.

The transition from traditional to mega-university is not just one of scale or technology. The new system removes the flexibility of the old one. There is a reduction in entropy—and this must be paid for. It is paid for by the development of university administrators. The new mega-universities require a greater skill input from the administrators as a whole; they make a greater demand that the university develop an overall strategy and co-ordination.

The traditional universities, such as Oxford and Cambridge in England or Bologna and Pisa in Italy, have the flexibility constantly to adjust their teaching and research directions to match the pace of the natural entropy vector. As a consequence, they have survived and thrived for hundreds of

Academic cocktails.

years—in this sense, few organisations can rival them. Traditional universities select their students from the populace using well-defined criteria and expect them to live on campus or at least within the university town. This is a well-defined system. By contrast, mega-universities tend to be less selective and have a disparate and distributed student population. This is more disordered, with the potential for an unacceptably high entropy vector. Success will occur only if suitable controls and skills are applied to modify the path to something close to the natural curve. The trade-off cost is this essential investment in training and managing.

Desirable redundancy

If you take flexibility out of a system, then you will need to compensate or to accept other limitations. We know this to be true for materials or physical structures. For example, change from a steel beam to a cast iron one. You may save money but the material is less flexible and will therefore be less able to withstand shock, which means that you might have to replace it more often or that it might break in use. Sometimes, for non-critical applications, the less flexible material may suffice; in other cases it can work out a lot more expensive in the long run.

A more high-tech example is carbon fibre composite materials which are beginning to replace aluminium for the skin of aircraft. Carbon fibre composites are lighter and stronger, but are more susceptible to damage from impacts such as the aircraft fitter dropping a spanner on it. The spanner would leave a visible dent in an aluminium skin, so you know it's there and can do something about it. The damage in the carbon fibre composite is inside the material and is just as potentially destructive, but nothing is visible to the naked eye. We must use sophisticated and expensive inspection techniques such as ultrasound, thermography and moiré to find and assess the damage. The net gain from the new material is complicated to assess; there are a number of trade-offs—'you can't have it just anyway you like it'.

The same is true for databases, where the objective should be effectiveness, not neatness. Building in some redundancy makes for an easier life. A perfectly inflexible system requires much greater skill at the design stage, including an ability to foresee future requirements and a much greater skill at operating the system to work within the constraints.

The hard disc on a computer is a classic example of a flexible system. Files are not stored neatly in lines like books in a library. When a file is deleted, it is not 'rubbed off' the disc. Instead, the computer operating system destroys the signpost to the file location on the disc. This is quicker than finding the location on the disc and removing the file. When you save a file, the operating system looks for the first area of the disc that it can find where there is no file or, more correctly, no signpost to that area, and writes the file to this area, writing over the previous occupant if necessary. If the file does not fit, then the operating system splits it up and puts the remainder in the next free location that it finds, and remembers all the signposts. This is a very flexible system but requires careful house-keeping and much thought at its inception.

So, perhaps it is time to draw these thoughts to a close. Just what point is being made here and how does it connect with anything? Well, in short, the simple point is that one needs to be aware of entropy trade-offs and we have tried to illustrate that you cannot change entropy without changing something else as well. And this simple truth not so much connects with anything as with everything. To repeat our paraphrase of the second law: 'you can't have it just anyway you like it'.

We have looked at the usually readily apparent trade-off between work done and entropy gain. We have also looked at the not-so-obvious trade-offs that require extra skill to support the new system or process (as varied as Watt's improvements to the steam engine, carbon fibre instead of aluminium or wider education access through distance learning) and the trade-off between entropy routes in a system. This latter point, which of course is the entropy vector, is well illustrated by our economics examples. Each company needs to make its own judgements and its own entropy balances, but recognising that the choices exist is the first step to making the good ones.

Notes and quotes

- Aubrey Wilson, said by some to be the 'UK father of industrial marketing', spent the second half of the twentieth century writing, lecturing and consulting in industrial or business-to-business marketing. The quote in the chapter was from *New Directions in Marketing: Business to Business Strategies for the 1990s* (Kogan Page, 1991). He claimed, as he had done on the previous nine occasions, that this would be his last book.
- Many books about the history of the Industrial Revolution will provide more information on Savery, Newcomen, Watt and Trevithick. We found that the approach taken by James Burke in *Connections* (Macmillan, London, 1978) highlighted the motivation for technological advances. Spot the trade-offs for yourself.

- Jacob Bronowski, *The Ascent of Man* (Science Horizons Inc., published by the British Broadcasting Corporation, 1973). On developing new ideas he asserts that 'the men who made the wild inventions and the grand ones came from the same mould'.
- 'Working Man's Burden', *The Economist*, Feb. 1999—based on research by Rafael Di Tella and Robert MacCulloch.
- Michael E. Porter, *Competitive Strategy* (The Free Press, London, 1980). Essential reading for all MBA students; best known for his analysis that the state of competition in an industry depends on five basic competitive forces and generic competing strategies (broad or focused, differentiated or cost).
- Charles Brian Handy, *The Hungry Spirit: Beyond Capitalism, a Quest for Purpose in the Modern World* (Hutchinson, London, 1997).
- Thomas A. Stewart, *Intellectual Capital: The New Wealth of Organisations* (Nicholas Brearley Publishing, London, 1998). The greater the human capital intensity of a business—that is, the greater its percentage of high-value-added work performed by hard-to-replace people—the more it can charge for its services and the less vulnerable it is to competitors.
- *Shakespeare's Complete Works*, edited by W.J. Craig (Oxford University Press, London, 1905). Just in case you don't want to wait for the troupe of monkeys with their alphabet blocks!

12

The Entropy Tool Kit

summary • pulling it all together • ideas and tools

In a final and brief chapter, we thought that we should select ten thoughts and ideas, tools if you like, that have been introduced in the book and just recap on them.

1. Tools

Now, don't get carried away with the idea of a tool. Entropy is not something that you can fix, or at least not permanently. We mentioned gardening in the introduction and gardening tools are probably the best analogy. Entropy is like your garden—naturally tending to disorder and prevented from so doing by your energetic efforts and the deployment of suitable tools. Tools will help create a pocket or two of order and by their skilful and co-ordinated use an attractive garden. But you need to buy good ones, look after them and use them correctly.

For 'garden' read 'company'. For 'tools' read 'equipment' and 'people'. And remember that everyone flourishes on praise and shrivels under criticism.

2. Space and time

For any system design, concentrate first on the time/velocity aspects and then consider issues of robustness, size, choice of materials. ... Or maybe concentrate first on issues of robustness, size, and choice of materials and then on the time/velocity aspects. Hey, with entropy at work you can't expect a definite rule. You can, however, expect to have greater disorder or, alternatively, greater expenditure of time, energy and money if you fail to separate the two dimensions and try to do the whole job at once.

3. Let the engine get hot

This is not a plea for inefficiency! It is, however, worth restating the simplicity of the second law. In normal, non-ideal systems, you cannot convert energy from one form to another without wasting some of it. And usually that waste appears as heat. The piston compresses a mixture of petrol vapour and air into the cylinder, the spark ignites it, the piston is driven and the car moves. But that is only part of the story. The cooling fluid needs also to circulate around the engine to limit the temperature by removing waste heat, otherwise the engine overheats and malfunctions. The combustion process can be optimised but there is always a residual level of waste, such as the energy loss in the exhaust gas. Engine designers know this, accept it and design for it. Designers of other systems need to remember the basic principles too. Always expect waste. Always plan to deal with it.

4. Redundancy

We looked at the issue of an over-constrained system in Chapter 3 when we discussed the arrangements at Detroit Airport. The concourse has more than its share of passengers fuming that they have missed their connection and the careful observer will see passengers trying to match Olympic qualifying times for the 200m in an effort to catch their planes. The cause of this distress and inefficiency is a system of gates and landing procedure that is too tightly constrained. Build in more gates than you need and the problem goes away. Of course, not many of us get the chance to design or manage airports and the cost of redundant gates will be huge, but the idea of built-in redundancy should not go away. For example, the cost of redundancy in a database is trivial and the value enormous.

5. Terrific upside, manageable downside

Entrepreneurs take risks but they are also skilful at avoiding them. Taking chances is a good way to increase the rate of disorder but the objective of an entrepreneur is not disorder but competitive advantage. Do some risk evaluation; careful focus and ruthless selection are the hallmarks of an entrepreneur. Set the entropy vector with care—or, as Richard Branson would have it, seek out opportunities that have a terrific upside and a manageable downside.

6. Course of least resistance

We argued at the outset that you should keep it simple because the effect of entropy would inevitably make things more complicated than you would hope. We also noted that 'going with the flow'—the course of least resistance—does not always get you to the desired destination. But sometimes it does and rather more often it takes you to an acceptable staging post. The course of least resistance is well trodden by wimps but that is not a good reason for rejecting it. If there is no value in having a battle and the destination of the least resistance course is acceptable, do not reject it. Of course, if it is not acceptable, don't! An incremental approach is recommended: remember, speed is relative and regular checking of direction helps to ensure that the desired destination is reached. Throughout this book, whenever we have introduced an equation, we have used the symbol 'S' to represent entropy. Ever wondered what the second S is in the 'KISS—keep it simple' slogan? It is S for entropy. It is there to remind you what the problem is.

7. Don't design for neatness

We used a number of military examples in the book and two more will serve us here. The British foot soldier of the eighteenth and nineteenth centuries looked magnificent in his bright uniforms with white criss-cross sashes across the breast. Very smart, very neat, but as warfare became more 'modern', not very practical. Would you wish to enter a sniper area with a big white 'X marks the spot' emblem on your chest? The second example might owe more to Hollywood than to history but there is no shortage of Western films depicting the Seventh Cavalry riding smartly and uniformly through the desert with their Indian scout out of ranks, out of uniform, out on his own. Fitting people into organisation charts might give neatness but it might not be fit for the purpose. If some of your people need different freedoms to do their jobs, then arrange it. Think 'organic', not 'organised', for organic organisations are those that are best able to manage change.

8. Get the right governors

It is easier, once you are in a company, to get the right governor in the James Watt sense of the word—that is, something that provides a controlling influence on your system so that you can have more flexible working arrangements. The sensible entropy vector is the one where you choose to build in some constraint to provide for greater efficiency. Always ask: What fail-safe mechanisms are built in to prevent my system (my company, my office, my factory) going out of control? Leave it up to chance or nature and you can rely on entropy giving you more disorder than you want.

Getting the right governor, as in 'boss', is also important. As a potential employee, we can choose at the interview stage, but how does a country get the right bosses for its businesses or indeed how does a big boss choose the littler bosses for his or her business? It is not as easy as ABC but we do suggest an analysis of alpha, beta and gamma managers on the basis of how energetic and efficient they are. We didn't include delta managers—you should seek to avoid them too. They might give you excitement but they are thin on effectiveness.

9. Manage perceptions

We can neither manage time nor save it. It is as relentless in its path as entropy in its. [Actually, entropy doesn't keep to a path; it sort of meanders off in unplanned directions.] What we can do to good effect is manage our perception of time. We can work towards sensible planning so that we do not skimp on preparation to save time, only to find it takes much more at a later and more critical stage. We can work towards a better-trained approach to how we manage our tasks and what targets we set ourselves so that we perceive effective achievement, leading to a virtuous circle of further planning and achievement, rather than the debilitating anxiety of underperformance that results from careless preparation and unrealistic targets. Much task management masquerades under the title of time management. There is more to 'time management' than just task management—you need to control the entropy vector too.

10. You can't have it any way you like it

It bears saying one last time. You have lots of choices but some things are not possible. Riding the entropy vector should help give you the wisdom to recognise the practicable from the unattainable. All improvements carry a new set of constraints; all attempts at the absolute will fail; all combinations of objectives will require compromise. And whilst on setting targets, remember that broad tolerances are as important as specific objectives. Finally, watch out for the expression 'all other things being equal'. They never are; the second law just will not permit such an ordered arrangement to exist.

11. Knowledge is negative entropy

We spent a great deal of time in the book talking of steam engines [some schoolboys never grow up] but we also noted the association of entropy with a lack of information. Whilst the usual emphasis is on information technology, we argue that it is knowledge management, not information technology, that is the key to success. Information must be acquired, ordered, assimilated and understood—in short, converted into knowledge—if it is to provide any real potential for useful work. As nations and individuals we need to commit resources and energy (exergy) to education, training and continuing development in order to make this conversion and to try to keep our mental entropy in check.

Note

Yes, we know there are eleven 'tools' and we only promised ten. Entropy, huh? It gets everywhere.

THE END

Index

Printed in the United States
By Bookmasters